Persuader-in-Chief

Global Opinion and Public Diplomacy in the Age of Obama

DR. NANCY SNOW

NIMBLE BOOKS LLC

ISBN-13: 978-1-934840-81-8

ISBN-10: 1-934840-81-5

Version 1.0; last saved 2009-01-15.

Nimble Books LLC

1521 Martha Avenue

Ann Arbor, MI 48103-5333

http://www.nimblebooks.com

The cover font, heading fonts and the body text inside the book are in Constantia, designed by John Hudson for Microsoft.

Contents

DEDICATION

For my brother Don

And for Melody

Angels, now

ABOUT THE AUTHOR

Nancy Snow is an American culture climatologist and persuasion/propaganda expert who blogs for The Huffington Post. She is Associate Professor of Public Diplomacy in the S.I. Newhouse School of Public Communications at Syracuse University, New York where she teaches and conducts research in the dual degree Masters in Public Diplomacy Program sponsored by the Newhouse School and Maxwell School for Citizenship and Public Affairs. She is Senior Fellow in the Center on Public Diplomacy at the University of Southern California's Annenberg School for Communication and is a lifetime member of the Public Diplomacy Council in Washington, D.C.

Snow was a Presidential Management Fellow with the United States Information Agency and State Department during President Bill Clinton's first term as well as a Fulbright scholar to Germany during Ronald Reagan's first term. She is an avid reader of presidential biographies and considers Ronald Reagan and Barack Obama the most fascinating rhetorical presidents to analyze, though she admires many of their predecessors including Jimmy Carter, JFK, FDR, TR, Abraham Lincoln and Thomas Jefferson.

Dr. Snow can trace her genealogy to Federalist Alexander Hamilton, Confederate President Jefferson Davis, and Mayflower passenger John Howland, as well as Native American tribes (Mohawk in New York and Creek in Alabama).

Snow is the author or editor of five other books, including the *Routledge Handbook of Public Diplomacy*. In 2006 she published *The Arrogance of American Power: What U.S. Leaders Are Doing Wrong and Why It's Our Duty to Dissent*. About that book, historian Howard Zinn said that "Nancy Snow writes with eloquence, passion, and crystal-clear prose" and "brings these qualities to the most important issue before our nation today: Why has the United States alienated people all over the world, and how can its citizens bring democracy alive to change national policy?" She is also the author of *Information War: American Propaganda, Free Speech and Opinion Control Since 9/11* and *Propaganda, Inc.: Selling America's Culture to the World*. She is editor with Yahya Kamilipour of *War, Media and Propaganda: A Global Perspective* that includes a foreword by Ben Bagdikian.

Dr. Snow received her Ph.D. in international relations (*magna cum laude*) from American University's School of International Service and B.A. in political science (*summa cum laude*) from Clemson University, South Carolina. Her award-winning doctoral dissertation, "Fulbright Scholars as Cultural Mediators," is being edited for future publication. She can be reached on Twitter, Facebook or at www.NancySnow.com.

IMPROVING US IMAGE ABROAD TOP PRIORITY FOR PRESIDENT OBAMA

(Originally published November 5, 2008 on The Huffington Post)

The U.S. Government Accountability Office (GAO in guvspeak) identified public diplomacy as one of 13 top priorities for President-elect Barack Obama.[1] Public diplomacy involves both state and non-state efforts to inform, influence, and engage overseas publics. The U.S. State Department leads the charge as our main agency of diplomacy, but State's expenditures on public diplomacy pale in comparison to those by the Department of Defense. This urgent call for improving America's image in the world and confronting the rise of anti-Americanism over the last five years is old news.

What we urgently need now, as GAO points out, is a core of properly trained public diplomats who can communicate well in an intercultural context. And we need abundant resources in order to run the best global persuasion programs. International broadcasting is our mainstay in public diplomacy, but think about it. What influences you? For me, it's a person I trust, someone who sits across the table from me in two-way dialogue and who I may end up collaborating with on some project. Listening to Radio Sawa or watching Al Hurra may reach a larger audience but won't engage people.

The election of Barack Obama was a positive step to help stem the tide of anti-Americanism but Obama's victory alone can't overcome all the resentment that has built up over the years. We Americans need to listen more, talk less, and truly engage people in a spirit of mutual understanding. It doesn't have to mean that we naively agree with each other on everything or hold hands across

---

[1] http://www.gao.gov/transition_2009/urgent/diplomacy-broadcasting.php

the oceans. It does mean that we need to acknowledge that we're in this global lifeboat together.

The U.S. Government Accountability Office (GAO) is an independent, nonpartisan agency that works for Congress. Often called the "congressional watchdog," GAO investigates how the federal government spends taxpayer dollars. The URL for the public diplomacy section includes previous reports by GAO over the years. I appreciate the work of this good government agency that cares about how we are spending our hard-earned public monies.

OBAMA: SOFT POWER, SMART POWER

(Originally published on The Huffington Post, November 11, 2008)

Setting an example is not the main means of influencing others; it is the only means.

—Albert Einstein

Two days after the election of Obama, I gave a talk on his likely foreign policy changes. I predicted that the era of GWOT (Global War On Terror) and GSAVE (Global Struggle Against Violent Extremism) is over. An Al Jazeera English report speculated as much.

This is not to say that the world suddenly got safer overnight. It's all in the approach and delivery, like a smooth pitch across the plate.

The world will no longer tolerate the Manichaean language of the Bush-Cheney years, the arrogance of power that led the United States to act unilaterally in so many areas and damn the public will in the process.

Yet what will replace it?

Some clues can be found at the Obama-Biden transition Web site Change.gov, which promises to restore American leadership in the world. The speculation now is that American exceptionalism may become archaic as the Obama administration calls on us to come together in a spirit of unity and attack problems in a post-partisan, globe-inclusive manner. Strictly leftwing or rightwing agendas won't serve this agenda well. Those of us who view ourselves as moderate independents may be the most satisfied with what comes out of the sausage factory, er, legislative process.

Michelle and Barack Obama checked out the new digs at 1600 Pennsylvania Avenue against a backdrop of deep pessimism. Despite the euphoria and enthusiasm surrounding the election results, a CNN poll reports that just 16 percent of those surveyed say things are going well in the country. That's an all-time low. Eighty-three percent say things are going badly, which is an all-time high.

We're known to the world as an almost naively optimistic nation, so these results go against type. Nevertheless, they reflect the damage that has been done to our national psyche, something that is not easily repaired, certainly not in a week's time. I think we're all overtired, feeling a dollar short and a day late. I wonder if our next persuader-in-chief can really pull off all those promises that won him the White House.

Mr. President-elect, get enough sleep, make sure you continue to work out everyday, and keep your family values intact. It's great to see the affection that you and your wife show. I can only imagine how difficult the road ahead is for you and your family.

And finally this: I read that Obama "thinks like a professor and inspires like a preacher." Thank goodness he doesn't inspire like a professor! The intellectual president follows the most uncurious president in my lifetime.

PERSUADER-IN-CHIEF: LOOKING BACK, MOVING FORWARD

Jesus loves the little children,
All the children of the world.
Red and yellow, black and white,
All are precious in His sight,
Jesus loves the little children of the world.

Clare Herbert Woolston, preacher from Chicago, Illinois

Nearly two years ago, I watched a 45-year-old junior Democratic Senator from Illinois give a speech on the steps of the former state Capitol in Springfield, Illinois. The weather was cold, in the single digits, as C-SPAN aired Senator Obama's announcement of his improbable run for the American presidency on February 10, 2007. Who does this guy think he is? At that time, I did not know how impressive his background was. Though still a young man, he had earned a Harvard law degree, served as the first African-American editor of the *Harvard Law Review*, taught constitutional law at the University of Chicago, and finished his undergraduate education at Columbia University in New York. He had written two best-selling books, *The Audacity of Hope: Thoughts on Reclaiming the American Dream* and *Dreams from My Father: A Story of Race and Inheritance*. He was just the third African-American elected to the U.S. Senate since Reconstruction.

How many of us could come close to his resume over a lifetime?

I'd like to say I could see it coming all along, but I did not. I figured Obama would burnish bright as a novelty candidate early on but then have a flameout moment like Howard Dean after the Iowa caucus. Hillary Clinton would arise like a phoenix from the ashes of what could have been. Better luck next time, we'd all say. He was too young, and it was too early. I sided with this *St. Petersburg Times* editorial: "Youthful optimism is admirable, but reality on the ground is a vicious, unforgiving tyrant. Obama needs more than one Senate term to qualify for the presidency of the United States. The world is too complex and dangerous for this likeable, charismatic, African-American neophyte to practice on-the-job training."[2] The writer, Bill Maxwell, noted that Obama's quick rise to prominence was because he had such a reassuring and polite manner, especially to white Americans. Consider this excerpt from *The Audacity of Hope*, in which Obama remarks about his campaign impressions of his fellow Americans, red and yellow black and white:

> *Not only did my encounters with voters confirm the fundamental decency of the American people, they also reminded me that at the core of the American experience are a set of ideals that continue to stir our collective conscience; a common set of values that bind us together despite our differences; a running thread of hope that makes our improbable experiment in democracy work. These values and ideals find expression not just in marble slabs of monuments or in the recitation of history books. They remain alive in the hearts and minds of most Americans - and can inspire us to pride, duty, and sacrifice.*

These are words of a man inspired by the content of character over the color of one's skin. Born to a white mother from Kansas and a black father from Kenya, his self-identity is African-American, though it too is fluid. "I am rooted in the African-American community. But I'm not defined by it. I am comfortable in my racial identity. But that's not all I am." He explained his embrace of the term African-American to the New York Times: "The reason that I've always been comfortable with that description is not a denial of my mother's side of the family. Rather, it's just a belief that the term African-American is by definition a hybrid term. African-Americans are a hybrid people. We're mingled with

---

[2] Bill Maxwell, "Senator, you better walk before you run," *St. Petersburg Times*, October 29, 2006.

African culture and Native American culture and European culture."

"If I was arrested for armed robbery and my mug shot was on the television screen, people wouldn't be debating if I was African-American or not. I'd be a black man going to jail. Now if that's true when bad things are happening, there's no reason why I shouldn't be proud of being a black man when good things are happening, too."

Regarding his biracial heritage, Steve Kroft of *60 Minutes* posed this challenge: "There are African-Americans who don't think that you're black enough, who don't think that you have had the required experience." Obama replied, "The truth of the matter is, you know, when I'm walking down the South Side of Chicago and visiting my barbershop, and playing basketball in some of these neighborhoods, those aren't questions I get asked."

"They think you're black," Kroft remarked, laughing. Obama: "As far as they can tell, yeah. I also notice when I'm catching a cab, nobody's confused about that either."[3]

I believe President Obama could get any cab he wants, though it likely won't be his preferred form of transportation.

The CBS news program *60 Minutes* profiled the candidate over two years, though it wasn't due to a newsroom hunch that they were covering the future forty-fourth president of the United States. It was because of his uniqueness as a candidate for the highest office in the land, in that "there had never been a presidential candidate quite like him—his last name rhymed with

---

[3] "The Road to the White House: First Steps, 60 Minutes Looks Back At The Early Days Of Obama's Run For The Presidency," *60 Minutes*, reported by correspondent Steve Kroft, December 26, 2008.

Osama, his middle name was Hussein; racially he was half white and half black, and politically he was green."[4]

Obama was also giving Hillary Clinton political migraines by running second in the national polls for the Democratic nomination for president.

Steve Kroft of *60 Minutes* asked Obama why him and why now. "Three years ago, you were a state legislator here in Springfield. What makes you think that you're qualified to be President of the United States?" Obama's reply was direct and yet at the time seemed over the top. "You know, I think we're in a moment of history where probably the most important thing we need to do is to bring the country together, and one of the skills that I bring to bear is being able to pull together the different strands of American life and focus on what we have in common."

In hindsight, those confident remarks were persuasive and symbolic. Obama's announcement was at the site of Lincoln's famous "House Divided" speech. Lincoln, like Obama, was an untested political neophyte whom many doubted could lead a nation.

Obama won't have to unify a nation on the need for a restoration project on America's reputation and image in the world. But all this good feeling cannot replace harsh realities he'll face. "President Obama may talk about change, 'smart power' ... and restoring America's reputation," says Anthony Cordesman, a former State and Defense department official now at the Center for Strategic and International Studies. "The fact remains, however, that he must deal with the foreign policy legacy from hell."[5]

---

[4] Steve Kroft, "*The Road to the White House: First Steps, 60 Minutes Looks Back At The Early Days Of Obama's Run For The Presidency.*"

[5] Richard Wolf, "Obama vows 'new dawn' with Clinton, Gates, Holder on team," *USA Today*, December 1, 2008.

His former Democratic rival and presumptive Democratic nominee for president will become the sixty-seventh Secretary of State. Senator Hillary Clinton pledges to expand the public diplomacy agenda. She vows to "reach out to the world again, seeking common cause and higher ground." In true smart power lingo, she added: "We know our security, our values, and our interests cannot be protected and advanced by force alone, nor, indeed, by Americans alone. We must pursue vigorous diplomacy using all the tools we can muster to build a future with more partners and fewer adversaries, more opportunities and fewer dangers, for all who seek freedom, peace and prosperity."[6] Clinton, like millions of others, believes that Barack Obama's election as president shows a "a new effort to renew America's standing in the world as a force for positive change."

---

[6] Stephen Kaufman, "Hillary Clinton Is Obama's Pick to Head State Department Senator pledges vigorous diplomacy to pursue freedom, peace and prosperity," America.gov, December 1, 2008.

BRAND OBAMA: THE 44TH PRESIDENT IS THE NEW FACE OF AMERICA IN THE WORLD

If there is anyone out there who still doubts that America is a place where all things are possible, who still wonders if the dream of our founders is alive in our time... tonight is your answer. Barack Obama, November 4, 2008

I am a child of the Sixties, just like the President-elect. We grew up in the Seventies and took on our adult responsibilities in the Eighties and beyond. Just knowing that this president was probably listening to a lot of the same R&B and Classic Oldies that I listened to growing up, I feel a natural affinity for Barack Obama as a person. I certainly don't know him and will likely never meet him, but I'm intrigued at what he symbolizes for America and its leadership in the world.

Barack Obama is the best marketing vehicle to come our way since the Marlboro Man, which is, according to *Advertising Age*, one of the most recognized American commercial symbols in the world. And now that he's given up smoking to win the presidency, he's a much healthier global symbol of America than that original rugged cowboy representing a product that, if used as directed, will shorten your life.

The Obama logo alone is the Nike swoosh of politics. Hillary Clinton had no match for it. She was the Microsoft PC to his Mac and we know which is cooler. Her pitiable response to Obama's freshness—that he was "frankly, naïve" about meeting with the heads of rogue nations didn't matter. Hillary Clinton in the primary season and later John McCain in the general election made the fatal mistake of believing that experience really did matter. In 2008 being a policy wonk from Washington was the political equivalent of being voted off early and into oblivion from American Idol.

Frank Rich said that Brand Obama may be the last best hope for restarting Brand America: "Barack Obama has little in common with George W. Bush, thank God, his obsessive workouts and message control notwithstanding. At a time when very few Americans feel very good about very much, Obama is generating huge hopes even before he takes office. So much so that his name and face, affixed to any product, may be the last commodity left in the marketplace that can still move Americans to shop."[7]

How does one fully capture the power of the brand that became Barack Obama, the president to succeed one of the most unpopular two-term presidents in modern history?

I was only peripherally aware of this junior Senator from Illinois until he won the Iowa Caucus and I began to think he might have an upstart's chance to dethrone the presumptive Democratic nominee for president, Hillary Clinton.

What reinforced his ability to win were two tipping points in the American psyche that occurred weeks apart but seemed as timely as to have been mastered by the best pageant event organizer. The first was Caroline Kennedy's January 2008 op-ed endorsement of Barack Obama in the *New York Times*. I was teaching opinion writing at Cal State Fullerton and part of my class preparation included culling examples of good opinion writing in the popular media. When I came across Kennedy's op-ed, I told my students that the op-ed was worth its weight in gold. It wasn't so much what she said in the body of the opinion piece or how eloquently she said it. In fact, her prose was quite pedestrian. What really mattered was the symbolism, the fact that it was Caroline Kennedy's byline and her obvious endorsement in the title of the piece, "A President Like My Father." To the junior senator from New York, Hillary Clinton, it had to be the equivalent of a stake to the heart. Two centuries later, the pen is still mightier than the sword!

---

[7] Frank Rich, "You're Likable Enough, Gay People," *The New York Times*, December 27, 2008.

Caroline Kennedy's last two paragraphs sealed the political passing of the baton:

> *I want a president who understands that his responsibility is to articulate a vision and encourage others to achieve it; who holds himself, and those around him, to the highest ethical standards; who appeals to the hopes of those who still believe in the American Dream, and those around the world who still believe in the American ideal; and who can lift our spirits, and make us believe again that our country needs every one of us to get involved.*
>
> *I have never had a president who inspired me the way people tell me that my father inspired them. But for the first time, I believe I have found the man who could be that president—not just for me, but for a new generation of Americans.*[8]

There is no such thing as a Royal Family in America, but the closest resemblance is the Kennedy family legacy. Two brothers ran for president, one won, and both saw their lives cut short by an assassin's bullet. John F. Kennedy and Robert Kennedy were involved in the turbulent civil rights issues of the 1960s. Years before Robert Kennedy's death in 1968, he gave an interview to the Voice of America in May 1961 when he was serving as Attorney General to his brother, the president. He predicted that the picture of America in racial turmoil would change in time. "There's no question that in the next thirty or forty years a Negro can also achieve the same position that my brother has as President of the United States, certainly within that period of time."[9] With some technical improvements, moving the date of the interview from 1961 to 1968 and dropping the thirty year reference altogether, the quote was popularized in 2008 as this: "There's no question about it. In the next 40 years a Negro can achieve the same position that my

---

[8] Caroline Kennedy, "A President Like My Father," *The New York Times*, January 27, 2008.

[9] "Crisis in Civil Rights," *Time*, June 2, 1961.

brother has."[10] Obama's DNA alone allowed some political communications and marketing specialists to present this candidate as the possibility of a supposed 1968 prediction as a 2008 dream fulfilled. A good brand marketing campaign must have a "wow" factor that increases the possibility of being involved in something of Nostradamus-like proportions.[11]

The second major tipping point was the Barack Obama Rock Star status in popular mass media. This wasn't a candidate just being analyzed within the pages of *Foreign Policy* or *Foreign Affairs* journals, both of which have an almost exclusively elite-level academic and policymaker audience. Obama was a man of the people and *People*, a candidate that could be as popular at any ObamaPalooza or gracing the pages with his beautiful wife and two daughters on the cover of *you name it* magazine.

The March 20, 2008 issue of *Rolling Stone* shows the earnest young face of one Barack Obama with the massive headline, "A New Hope." Obama had lost the California primary in February but he was winning the marketing race, helped along by that other arms race in politics called fundraising. Below the Obama headline was the prescient header in much smaller font: "Hillary's Last Stand." Any commuter just glancing at this magazine cover would know what that implied. Hillary Rodham Clinton was doomed. The young, fresh, hopeful and intelligent man of change had just ridden to town on his own black and white horse. He was truly incomparable and made Hillary Clinton and her pantsuits look oh so 1990s Lane Bryant.

Jann Wenner, publisher of *Rolling Stone* gushed off the pages of his magazine in his personal endorsement:

---

[10] "And Still They Rise," Irishabroad.com, November 12, 2008.
[11] See "Forty Years" on Snopes.com, http://www.snopes.com/politics/obama/kennedy.asp.

> *The tides of history are rising higher and faster these days. Read them right and ride them, or be crushed. And then along comes Barack Obama, with the kinds of gifts that appear in politics but once every few generations. There is a sense of dignity, even majesty, about him, and underneath that ease lies a resolute discipline. It's not just that he is eloquent—with that ability to speak both to you and to speak for you—it's that he has a quality of thinking and intellectual and emotional honesty that is extraordinary.*[12]

In summer 2008 I heard about "Baracksteady," one of the hot-selling buttons and T-shirts at the Democratic Convention in Denver. There is even a Web site to go with the merchandise: http://baracksteady.ytmnd.com/. The song is to the music of the Whispers' "Rock Steady," circa 1987. Rocksteady is a Jamaican dance style from the 1960s that inspired reggae.

At the time I learned about "Baracksteady," I reacted negatively with a sense that we have finally come to this: The total manufacturing and branding of a presidential candidate. It seemed that Barack Obama's slogan "Yes We Can!" wasn't too far removed from Robert Redford's character Bill McKay ("For a better way: Bill McKay!") in the 1972 film, *The Candidate*. The late great actor Peter Boyle played McKay's political consultant, Marvin Lucas, to whom McKay turns to after his victory party and says, "Marvin, what do we do know?" Marvin doesn't answer. He has no answer, because his work is done. This film, reflective of the political cynicism of the early 1970s, shows a desperate candidate anxious about actually having to govern after he has been manufactured like ice cream.

So one has to wonder now. Which came first? The iconography of Baracksteady to placate the celebrity aspect of Barack Obama's candidacy, or was it Obama's steady and cool handling of the international spotlight, such as his very presidential speech in Berlin:

---

[12] Jann S. Wenner, "A New Hope," *Rolling Stone*, March 20, 2008, 35.

I come to Berlin as so many of my countrymen have come before. Tonight, I speak to you not as a candidate for President, but as a citizen -- a proud citizen of the United States, and a fellow citizen of the world.

I know that I don't look like the Americans who've previously spoken in this great city. The journey that led me here is improbable. My mother was born in the heartland of America, but my father grew up herding goats in Kenya. His father—my grandfather—was a cook, a domestic servant to the British.

At the height of the Cold War, my father decided, like so many others in the forgotten corners of the world, that his yearning—his dream—required the freedom and opportunity promised by the West. And so he wrote letter after letter to universities all across America until somebody, somewhere answered his prayer for a better life.

No one then in July 2008 could have with 100 percent certainty predicted that this man who would be the leader of the free world would actually go on to become the 44th president of the United States. But his words, that he didn't look like Americans before him—John Kennedy, Ronald Reagan, were misleading. He is America, as surely as California is America or New York is America.

As First Lady of California Maria Shriver said about Obama when she, along with Caroline Kennedy and Oprah Winfrey, endorsed him in California: "The more I thought about it, I thought, you know, if Barack Obama were a state, he'd be California: diverse, open, smart, independent, bucks tradition, innovative, inspiring, dreamer, leader."

Though Obama did not win the California primary, he laid the foundation for a big win in the general. One of out four voters in California's Democratic primary was Latino. Obama secured the endorsement of the *Los Angeles Times*, in whose media market 60 percent of all Latino voters reside and of *La Opinion*, a leading Latino newspaper in that state.

California's population is 60.9% White American, 6.1% Black or African American, 12.4% Asian American, 16.4% other races, 0.7% American Indian, 3.1% mixed race. Over one-third (35.5%) are Hispanic or Latino (of any race). 43.3% of the population is non-Hispanic white. That Obama state, California, is home to the fifth largest population of African-Americans in the United States, an estimated 2,163,530 residents. California's Asian population is estimated at 5 million, approximately one-third of the nation's 14.9 million Asian Americans. California's Native American population of 376,093 is the most of any state. The state of California has the largest minority population in the United States, making up 57% of the state population. Obama is very much an American brand icon. America is under the 44th president of the United States "the world's home away from home."

This America is the brand land of commercialism and self-promotion, so upon further reflection I see now that these Barack Obama commercial tie-ins made sense. This powerful marketing machine was necessary not only for him to win but also to make a lasting connection between himself as a powerful emotional symbol for change and hope, and for a nation of people and citizens of the world to emulate. This child of the Sixties knew that to win hearts and minds you need to capture the audience's attention through positive association, and what is more powerful than visual and audio association that makes people want to jump to their feet? Give the people something to dance to in times of trouble. If nothing else, you've got to give us children of the 60s and 70s our props when it comes to some good dance music.

As an academic, I've had the privilege to teach during long stretches of national political contests or international strife. When the economic and political times are not usually good at the macro level, the level of interest and involvement from students in the classroom often ticks upward. My first teaching opportunity while still a doctoral student was an introduction to peace and conflict resolution at American University in Washington, D.C. It coincided with Desert Shield, the lead-in mobilization to what we quickly called the "CNN War" or Desert Storm. I recall having ROTC students and peace-loving anti-war students. I invited both pro- and anti-war guest lecturers whose only requirement was to be themselves and to tell the truth as they knew it. I did not direct the dialogue but offered up their perspectives so that students could draw their own conclusions and think for themselves.

I try at times to remain emotionally detached and nonpartisan about hotly-contested political contests, the hottest to the touch being the election of the American president. I do this so that I can avoid becoming a proselytizer by elevating my own or anyone's ideological or partisan positions.

I'm not always very successful at this detachment. I'm a public scholar. I make my living observing and writing about the political communications environment and most of what I have to say is strongly opinionated and judgmental. I share my observations and perspectives with broader and more diverse publics beyond the academy through blogging, posting on my Web site, giving public lectures, and engaging with other souls on social networking sites like Facebook. When I do a radio, print or television interview, the moderators or reporters aren't satisfied with a mushy middle-of-the-road type answer. They seek out public scholars to add subjective interpretation of events. Once my students become aware of my public scholarship, they are generally not satisfied with a "no comment" about all things politics.

So here is my strongest conclusion from this historic presidential election from one who observes politics and communications.

Brand Obama has trumped Brand America. Barack Obama's candidacy from the time he gave his memorable speech, "The Audacity of Hope" at the 2004 Democratic Convention to his Victory speech in Grant Park Chicago on November 4, 2008 was a triumph in marketing a relatively obscure political neophyte into a figure whose visage is likely to grace Mount Rushmore someday.

Obama became the most iconic American president since Abraham Lincoln and John F. Kennedy. As Mathew Creamer of *Advertising Age* observed:

> *Using his strong rhetorical skills, he spoke with John F. Kennedy's vocabulary of change and renewal translated into a master narrative reminiscent of Ronald Reagan's "Morning in America," all the while evincing Bill Clinton's talent for forging human connections. Even Ross Perot's imprint was felt in Mr. Obama's late-in-the-game prime-time infomercial shown in a seven-network roadblock, except this time the homely, big-eared, white guy crunching numbers was replaced with a handsome, big-eared, black guy delivering a much-more- appropriate-for-prime-time message.*[13]

This presidential election cycle college age students were more energized than they had been in decades. Politico.com reported that "President-elect Barack Obama's 34-point margin of victory with voters under 30 was the largest in a generation, cut across lines of class, color and education—and [became] the most impressive youth mandate in modern American history... Sixty-six percent of voters under age 30 preferred Obama while just 32 percent favored McCain—nearly four times the size of John F. Kennedy's lead with the group in 1960, which led him to famously declare in his inaugural address that 'the torch has been passed to a new generation of Americans.'"[14]

The day after the election, we all returned to our daily lives. My new normalcy was to teach two public diplomacy classes at Syracuse University's Newhouse School. One student from China asked if I were going to put Obama's win into perspective during class time. Even though we had plenty of other topics to cover as outlined in the syllabus, I promised that I would, knowing that the

---

[13] Matthew Creamer, "Barack Obama and Audacity of Marketing," *Adage.com*, November 10, 2008.

[14] "Obama has historic youth mandate," www.Politico.com, November 8, 2008.

students wanted to share their reactions. There was a central theme that day. They kept saying that America is back, they were proud of their country's decision on November 4, and are proud to be Americans more than ever. My Chinese student said that she felt proud for America and that it was now okay in her eyes for Americans to be proud. The last eight years had been a time of apologies and missteps and to her we had now redeemed ourselves with the filling in of our collective ballot sheets.

Barack Obama's biography, DNA, and rhetoric opens up so many possibilities, including the ability to wear two hats as American citizens but also global diplomats. It occurred to me on that day that we may very well be seeing the beginnings of presidential leadership that co-inspires mutual trust instead of conspires to undermine public will. I couldn't help but notice that the Google News Web site had what seemed like hundreds of articles about the global goodwill coming out of the decisive Obama victory. It is as if the world's arms were embracing us, perhaps for a moment in time, but possibly in preparation for something truly transformative in American foreign policy.

Obama's victory speech on November 4 was beyond anything Bill Clinton could have delivered in 1992:

> *And to all those watching tonight from beyond our shores, from parliaments and palaces to those who are huddled around radios in the forgotten corners of our world—our stories are singular, but our destiny is shared, and a new dawn of American leadership is at hand. To those who would tear this world down—we will defeat you. To those who seek peace and security—we support you. And to all those who have wondered if America's beacon still burns as bright—tonight we proved once more that the true strength of our nation comes not from our the might of our arms or the scale of our wealth, but from the enduring power*

of our ideals: democracy, liberty, opportunity, and unyielding hope.[15]

As I listened I thought back to my first book, *Propaganda, Inc.: Selling America's Culture to the world*. It was a play on the United States Information Agency motto, "telling America's story to the world." As a cultural affairs specialist at the agency from 1992-1994, I recall thinking that it is America's diverse stories, not the official story about America, that is our best advertising campaign to the world. Why just tell one? And along comes one Barack Obama who embodies that philosophy.

As *Newsweek International* editor Fareed Zakariah said after the election on November 4, 2008:

> *Americans seem to understand that bloviating about 'USA as Number One' is cheap rhetoric, divorced from the real world. They sense that the real challenge for Washington is not to boast about America's might but to use its capacities—military, political, intellectual—to work with others to create a more stable, peaceful and prosperous world in which American interests and ideals will be secure.*[16]

We're One Among Many Ones may be this nation's new smart power motto.

---

[15] Barack Obama, "A World That Stands as One," *Spiegel Online International*, July 24, 2008.

[16] Fareed Zakariah, "McCain's Downfall: Republican Foreign Policy," www.fareedzakariah.com, November 9, 2008.

McCAIN FAILS TO PERSUADE

(Originally published on The Huffington Post October 8, 2008 as "The Democratic Candidate Turns Persuader")

Sweetness in the air, and justice on the wind,
laughter in the house where the mourners had been.
The deaf shall have music, the blind have new eyes,
the standards of death taken down by surprise.
Alleluia, the great storm is over, lift up your wings
and fly!
Alleluia, the great storm is over, lift up your wings
and fly!

From "Alleluia, The Great Storm Is Over" by Bob Franke
©1982 Telephone Pole Music Publishing Co. (BMI)
Used by permission.

This isn't a stretch. I can see clearly now. SAFIH (Stick a Fork in Him). McCain is done. Senator Barack Obama will be the 44th president of the United States of America. This is not an endorsement but a prediction. Of course, I'm the same person who predicted John Kerry would win in 2004.

I'm much more sure of my prediction this time.

Last time I thought the youth vote would tilt the election in Kerry's favor. But the youth didn't turn out as predicted. Plus, they weren't really all that enamored of Kerry. The youth vote in 2008 is all Obama, all the time. College campuses, with few exceptions, are Obama Central.

It doesn't take a village to raise the white flag on the McCain-Palin ticket. It takes a disappointing showing by Senator John McCain in Round Two of the presidential debates.

Senator Barack Obama, aka known as "that one" by Senator McCain, erased lingering doubts that he isn't ready for the Prime Time Presidency.

Senator McCain raised more doubts that he has the energy or interest in the job. His point of no return occurred at the time he declared he was suspending his presidential campaign in order to focus on the economic bailout in Washington. That putting country first utterance was supposed to come across as presidential. Instead it came across as unsteady. It's been downhill ever since for the McCain-Palin Straight Talk buggy and the ride has been bumpy, although Governor Sarah Palin still has that Energizer™ snow-bunny aura about her. (I want to know what daily multivitamin she takes.) Since the old military man seems unwilling or unable to return fire, he has left it to Palin to question Obama's Facebook-like credentials. It's not sticking. The guilt-by-association tactics and radical community organizer labels are backfiring as characteristics of a campaign in freefall.

The world is not only watching, but it is weighing in. We're being told, "Hey America, give this guy from Illinois a chance. We like him." In ordinary times global public opinion wouldn't count as much. But these are extraordinary times and this time the world is a Blue State.

Have the mainstream media assisted Obama in making his case to America? Of course they have. But Senator Obama had the same media format as Senator McCain in Mississippi and Tennessee, so the charges against the media aren't persuasive this time.

There was once a time when I watched in awe as Senator John McCain kept Town Hall crowds spellbound with his inspirational rhetoric. It was New Hampshire and a long eight years ago.

HEY WORLD, HOW DO YOU LIKE US NOW?

(Originally published on The Huffington Post November 5, 2008)

Figure 1. New York Times ad on Guantanamo (American Civil Liberties Union).

And they say newspapers are dead in America. The *New York Times* sold out after printing 275,000 extra copies. People were seen standing in line outside the NY Times headquarters at 41st and Eighth Avenue in New York. Nowadays it's hard to give away newspapers for free. But today is when displaying the results on Google News isn't going to cut it. We need that hard copy to make it real and to store away for our grandchildren. I was there, we can share. I witnessed America say a collective "Yes!"

For many Americans, the other guy didn't win. They feel a sense of loss. An aging American hero who energized his own base of mavericks in 2000 won the nomination of his political party in 2008, but not the hearts and minds of the general electorate. Senator McCain, you inspired me eight years ago. I don't know where that Senator went in 2008. I never felt uplifted by your rhetoric. Joe the Plumber drove me crazy. It wasn't your year. It never could have been.

We made a mistake in 2004. And we had to correct that mistake yesterday.

We said we were sorry in 2004. Global friends, today we display a sense of pride about America, some of us for the first time, some in a long time. We're having our Michelle Obama moment.

Where do we go from here? Do GWOT and GSAVE become outmoded acronyms? Recall the Global War on Terror and Global Struggle Against Violent Extremism. Will the Obama Effect translate into a transformative, life-affirming diplomacy? Today we think it will. Only tomorrow will tell.

For now, my students are excited and enthusiastic. They keep saying America is back, that they are proud to be Americans, and that Obama's win allows them to wear two hats as American citizens but also global citizen diplomats.

We may be seeing the beginnings of presidential leadership that co-inspires mutual trust instead of conspires to undermine public will. We may actually start bowling together, instead of alone.

Obama's acceptance speech was beyond anything the Democratic persuader-in-chief Bill Clinton could have delivered in 1992:

So let us summon a new spirit of patriotism; of service and responsibility where each of us resolves to pitch in and work harder and look after not only ourselves, but each other. Let us remember that if this financial crisis taught us anything, it's that we cannot have a thriving Wall Street while Main Street suffers – in this country, we rise or fall as one nation; as one people.

> *Let us resist the temptation to fall back on the same partisanship and pettiness and immaturity that has poisoned our politics for so long. Let us remember that it was a man from this state who first carried the banner of the Republican Party to the White House – a party founded on the values of self-reliance, individual liberty, and national unity. Those are values we all share, and while the Democratic Party has won a great victory tonight, we do so with a measure of humility and determination to heal the divides that have held back our progress. As Lincoln said to a nation far more divided than ours, "We are not enemies, but friends...though passion may have strained it must not break our bonds of affection." And to those Americans whose support I have yet to earn – I may not have won your vote, but I hear your voices, I need your help, and I will be your President too.*

Like Ben and Jerry's Coffee Heath Bar Crunch, this guy is almost too good to be true.

IT'S A SMALLER WORLD, AFTER ALL

The presidential election of Barack Obama on November 4, 2008 was the political equivalent of a major seismic event in shifting attitudes and opinions forward about America's leadership, place, and reputation in the world.

No doubt, America is back.

"If there is anyone out there who still doubts that America is a place where all things are possible," said Obama to the several hundred thousands in Chicago's Grant Park after winning the presidential election, "tonight is your answer."

The BBC reported what an Obama win meant for the United Kingdom. "The power of the US president is felt in the UK and all over the globe. That's why Americans like to call him "The Leader of the Free World." In symbolism alone, the win was substantial. "For the first time ever, the most important person in the world is black. Or at least of mixed racial origin. His mother is white and his father grew up herding goats in an African village. When you consider it's only a few decades since black school children were officially banned from white schools in the US, it shows how much both America and the world have changed."

Gideon Rose, managing editor of *Foreign Affairs* magazine, said that Obama's style and substance alone are enough to "reboot" America's foreign policy. "This is the America that foreigners read about, they can't quite believe exists, and they love to see. It's the America of movies, TV. It's the America that is the truly global country that can lead the world to make it what it could be."

Rose says that with this election of a new president, America has "lived up to its own reputation, its own principles." The world feels like it's gotten Kennedy in style, substance, and charisma and a Lincoln or Truman in serious policy competence and intelligence.

Obama may have been sold on style as a presidential candidate but as president-elect, the world sees more of his substance emerging.

The day after the election, *New York Times* reporter Ethan Bronner shared global reaction in his article, "For Many Abroad, an Ideal Renewed." Quite simply, the world over was overwhelmed with excitement and relief. Reporting from the Gaza Strip, Bronner wrote, "From far away, this is how it looks: There is a country out there where tens of millions of white Christians, voting freely, select as their leader a black man of modest origin, the son of a Muslim. There is a place on Earth—call it America—where such a thing happens."

"Mr. Obama's election offers most non-Americans a sense that the imperial power capable of doing such good and such harm—a country that, they complain, preached justice but tortured its captives, launched a disastrous war in Iraq, turned its back on the environment and greedily dragged the world into economic chaos—saw the errors of its ways over the past eight years and shifted course. They say the country that weakened democratic forces abroad through a tireless but often ineffective campaign for democracy—dismissing results it found unsavory, cutting deals with dictators it needed as allies in its other battles—was now shining a transformative beacon with its own democratic exercise."

British historian Tristam Hunt says that President-elect Barack Obama "brings the narrative that everyone wants to return to—that America is the land of extraordinary opportunity and possibility, where miracles happen."

"But some remain darkly suspicious of the election itself. They doubted that Mr. Obama could be nominated or elected. Now they doubt that he will govern. The skeptics say they believe that American policy is deeply institutionalized and that if Mr. Obama tries to shift it, 'they'—the media, the corporate robber barons, the hidden powers—will box him in or even kill him."

"There is a risk, however, to all the extraordinary international attention paid to this most international of American politicians: Mr. Obama's focus will almost certainly be on the reeling domestic economy, housing and health care. Will he be able even to lift his head and gaze abroad to all those with such high expectations?"

With the exception of Israel, Georgia and the Philippines that leaned Senator John McCain's way, Obama seemed to have the entire world supporting his victory.

Obama's victory signifies an enormous positive shift in attitudes and opinions toward the United States. But it also represents a paradox of American power. The era of American exceptionalism may be over. Bronner writes: "The world's view of an Obama presidency presents a paradox. His election embodies what many consider unique about the United States—yet America's sense of its own specialness, of its destiny and mission, has driven it astray. They want Mr. Obama, the beneficiary and exemplar of American exceptionalism, to act like everyone else, only better, to shift American policy and somehow to project both humility and leadership."

GLOBAL OPINION MATTERS: A NEW DAY IN AMERICA?

This essay is based on a talk to the Association of Public Diplomacy Scholars at the University of Southern California, March 22, 2007, and carried live in C-SPAN)[18]

On Tuesday, February 27, 2007, the Gallup organization released its annual survey of how Americans view world affairs. Trust in the federal government to handle foreign affairs, where Karen Hughes is employed, is at its lowest point in ten years. Just a little over a third of us (37%) satisfied with the position of the United States in the world , the lowest reading that Gallup has polled on this measure since 1962. This compares to 71% who were satisfied in the months following the Sept. 11 terrorist attacks, and 69% who were satisfied just after the Iraq War began in March 2003. By March 2008, Americans' discontent with the U.S. position in the world had reached a record-high level.

What a difference a few years can make.

From 2000-2004, Gallup found that a majority of Americans believed that other nations held us in favor. In the months after September 11th, 75% of Americans thought that foreign leaders respected President Bush. From 2004 to 2007, Americans believed the opposite. Only 21% of Americans now believe that foreign leaders have respect for our president. I'd love to know the news consumption patterns of those twenty-one percent, wouldn't you?! This is the worst reading on this question since it was first asked about Clinton in 1994. This is not a statistic that gives me

[18] References:http://www.gallup.com/poll/26707/Americans-Pessimistic-About-US-Role-World.aspx
http://www.gallup.com/poll/104782/Discontent-US-Global-Position-Hits-Record-High.aspx

schadenfreude. I respect the office of the president and am sorry about the loss.

Just look at the executive leadership in Washington. I don't even have time to go into Congress, which given its best opportunity cannot even censure this president. Bush and Cheney are masters are putting a "good face" on disasters. When the British government announced it was withdrawing up to 1,600 troops in the next several months, Vice President Dick Cheney told ABC News' Jonathan Karl: "Well, I look at it and see it is actually an affirmation that there are parts of Iraq where things are going pretty well." Cheney's Kool-aid drinking buddy is White House Press Secretary Tony Snow (No, there's no relation!) When a reporter asked Tony Snow: "The Iraq withdrawal plan announced by Tony Blair, do you see that as a negative sign?" Snow responded: "No, it indicates that there's been some progress in Basra ... the fact that they [the British] have made some progress on the ground is going to enable them to move some of the forces out." Tonight I'd like to ask Tony Snow to stop using the verb version of our namesake when discussing the disastrous state of affairs in Iraq.

Only about a third of the American public agrees with the positive spin of these men. When asked for their views on the British troop withdrawal, 65% of Americans interviewed in a Feb. 22-25, 2007 Gallup Poll Panel study say it is a sign things are going poorly, rather than well. Just 3 in 10 agree with Dick Cheney and Tony Snow.

And yet, who does the White House call on to explain American policy and values to the world? Figure skaters like Michelle Kwan and ex-broadcast journalists and White House Iraq Group members like Karen Hughes. I'll get to Kwan in a minute.

Hughes is not known for her foreign policy prowess but for guard-dog like devotion to President George W. Bush. While a professor of political science at New England College, I also served as executive director of Common Cause of New Hampshire, a part-time devotional duty in service to citizen activism. At a 2000 rally, I was within a ten foot pole from Hughes in Concord, New Hampshire when Bush was campaigning in the first-in-the-nation presidential primary. She made a strong impression that I just might be zapped into vapor if I got too close to then Governor Bush when Hughes was around as his unofficial governor-in-chief bodyguard. Luckily I kept my distance and remain intact today. She was certainly good at protecting Bush far from the madding crowds, a tactic that failed to win the hearts and minds of many New Hampshire voters as we mass exited for John McCain's straight talk and open door Town Hall policy.

With some irony, Hughes was tasked with promoting a more open dialogue between our nation and overseas publics. Shortly after 9/11, Hughes earned her information warfare stripes while heading the White House day-to-day duties of the Coalition Information Centers (CIC) that coordinated the message of the day from London to Washington to Islamabad during the bombing raids over Afghanistan. She was identified then as one of the main players in what the *New York Times* called the largest communications war effort since World War II.

Hughes is credited with massaging Bush's "compassionate conservative" moniker. During the buildup to war in Iraq, Hughes was part of the *White House Iraq Group*, which coordinated strategy for selling the war to the American people. Previously, she coordinated government information from Kabul to London in the newly created war on terror. Hughes took the job previously held by Charlotte Beers, in which she was responsible for improving the way the U.S. is perceived in other countries, including the Muslim and Arab world.

At the time of her appointment in September 2005, Hughes held a Town Hall meeting for State Department employees in which she described her plans to improve US image abroad in militaristic phrases, outlining a "rapid-response unit" and "forward-deploy regional SWAT teams" to "formulate a more strategic and focused approach to all our public diplomacy assets." The *Washington Post*'s Dana Milbank reported: "One of her underlings rose to ask how this effort squared with the administration's famously tight control over its message. ... Hughes replied that ambassadors are free to talk—if they use the talking points she sends them. 'If they make statements based on something I sent them,' she said, 'they're not going to be called on the carpet.'"

On November 8, 2006, Elizabeth Williamson of the *Washington Post* published "Karen's Rules on Diplomacy: Talk to the Media—if You Dare: Hughes Sends Memo on Getting the Word to the World. The memo was sent to all consular and diplomatic posts who speak on the record. Among the rules was the following: Rule #5: "Don't Make Policy. This is a sensitive area about which you need to be careful. Do not get out in front of USG policymakers on an issue, even if you are speaking to local press. When in doubt on a policy shift, seek urgent guidance from your regional hub, public affairs or your regional public diplomacy office. Use your judgment and err on the side of caution."

So what would Hughes have the diplomats, much less the American people focus on? If not policy, then what? Hughes penned an article for the State Department "E-Journal" (http://usinfo.state.gov/journals/). Her paradigm for public diplomacy? "Waging Peace." Three priorities in this include that America must continue to be the beacon of hope for the rest of the world. Secondly, the U.S. seeks to isolate and marginalize the violent extremists who threaten the civilized world and confront their ideology of tyranny and hate with the U.S. message of respect for the contributions and cultures of others. Third, the U.S. seeks to nurture the common values and common interests that the U.S. has with the world. "What we are seeking to do with public diplomacy—nurture the sense that Americans and people of different countries, cultures, and faiths have much more in common than the issues that divide us."

Now on to Michelle Kwan.

Michelle Kwan, as you might imagine, has much to say about improving the way the U.S. is perceived in the Muslim and Arab world. I'm kidding, of course. Kwan was named "America's First Public Diplomacy Ambassador" in November 2006. The 26-year old five time world champion who vaulted onto the world figure skating stage at 15 was a graduate student in political science and international relations at the University of Denver, alma mater of Secretary of State Condoleezza Rice. Kwan seems like a good safe choice to represent U.S. values in diversity and sports excellence. She won't be bothered with policy discussions. From all I've seen of Kwan in the media, she seems a warm and gracious person and will likely do us proud.

However I'm not sure if she alone can clean up the mess we've made by linking public diplomacy to the Bush war on terror.

As Martha Bayles wrote in *The Sun*: "Today, the chief messages of U.S. public diplomacy—that to fight terrorism, America must occupy Iraq, restrict visas, and suspend legal protections for both prisoners and citizens—are seen as 'big lies' by millions of people around the world. We can keep repeating this message, or we can change tack. Either way, our purpose is not well served by political correctness, on the left or on the right."

Despite a blue-tilting Congress and the resignation of Rumsfeld, the proof of our unpopular foreign policies in the world continues unabated.

I elect to nominate my own candidate who provides a face of the United States in the world that is decidedly politically incorrect. He may not have been the first person Dr. Rice or Karen Hughes thought of to help improve our image in the world. Actually, I'm sure he wasn't even on their Top 10 list. I'd like to think he is equally competent to Ms. Kwan to handle the ambassadorial duties. He holds a Ph.D. from Columbia University, is a WWII veteran, and his resume includes countless random and purposive acts of representing the oft-touted U.S. values of free speech, free press, and social justice. He's neither left nor right, but a radical (getting at the roots) truth-teller about why our national image remains checkered.

He is Howard Zinn, author of the million-seller *A People's History of the United States and You Can't Be Neutral on a Moving Train*. He wouldn't teach figure skating, maybe citizen activism and dissent. Wars, not peace, and their subsidiaries, profits, not people, are seen as the eternal American values in the eyes of the world. People ambassadors like Zinn advocate a life-affirming and dignified option.

Prof. Zinn makes us ask critical questions: How many of us really wanted to go to war with Iraq? How many of us cringed when we saw Secretary of State Colin Powell do his show-and-tell presentation to the United Nations, a speech that he later deeply regretted? How many of us shuddered in fear from what then National Security adviser Rice said was the possibility of a "mushroom cloud" over Iraq if we didn't act soon enough?

The Bush 48-hour ultimatum speech to Saddam Hussein was as much an ultimatum on our humanity.

We can't be all that surprised that our presence in Iraq perpetuates U.S. unpopularity in that region, much less the world. Deep down we know that this war on terror has only increased terror. How many of us remain afraid to speak out against perpetual war and violence in the name of peace, humanitarianism and nonviolence? Why is war the patriotic American value and dissent against war subversive?

Do we want to be known as the military superpower or the humanitarian superpower? If we prefer humanitarian, then we cannot count on any one election to change our image from feared superpower to beloved exemplar of what's right, honorable, and just.

We're still under (pre)occupation as a people led to a war of choice by a now discredited wartime president. We're still sending men and women volunteers to Iraq to fight for what they're told, and often repeat, is our country's security and safety. The commander in chief of those armed forces says we're fighting the war "over there" so we don't have to fight it here at home. However self-serving that explanation, the soldiers are also fighting for military-industrial profits and a failed policy that has killed mostly non-combatant civilians. The so-called good war, this isn't. And in the homeland, we're now subject to a new insecurity, the just passed Military Commission Act, which makes all of us potential unlawful enemy combatants in this continuing war on terror.

In a column Zinn wrote for *The Progressive* just days after September 11, 2001, he said:

> *We need new ways of thinking. A $300 billion dollar military budget has not given us security. Military bases all over the world, our warships on every ocean, have not given us security. Land mines and a "missile defense shield" will not give us security. We need to rethink our position in the world. We need to stop sending weapons to countries that oppress other people or their own people. We need to decide that we will not go to war, whatever reason is conjured up by the politicians or the media, because war in our time is always indiscriminate, a war against innocents, a war against children. War is terrorism, magnified a hundred times.*

He wrote those words before the failed war policy, the death and destruction of so many fellow global citizens, and before a military budget request for FY 2007 of over $500 billion. We need not wonder why just days before this election the British public declared itself in one poll as more in fear of the American president's threat to world peace than either North Korea or Iran.

Let's send a positive message of hope, activism, and the spirit of redemption to a world that still fears us a lot more than it admires those American values now being packaged by Washington.

Hillary Rodham Clinton, the once presumptive Democratic nominee, said something very prescient in 2002 when she supported the President's call for the use of force against Iraq. Here's how she explained her vote: "My vote, is not, however, a vote for any new doctrine of preemption, or for unilateralism, or for the arrogance of American power or purpose—all of which carry grave dangers for our nation, for the rule of law and for the peace and security of the people throughout the world."

"If we're an arrogant nation, they'll resent us," President Bush said in his second debate with Al Gore in 2000. "If we're a humble nation, but strong, they'll welcome us." He was more right than ever. Can we imagine it now? America, the Gentle Giant. But instead we've seen foreign policy the last 8 years ala Frank Sinatra's "My Way" or the highway. The wonderful Washington Post columnist Mary McGrory referred to us once as the "SUV of nations," hogging the road, guzzling our gas, and alienating our fellow road travelers in the process. Others disdain for us means that when we need to lead, we cannot. A leader who has lost the respect of his subordinates and his confidants is a leader no more.

Is it possible in the age of Obama for the United States to now rule without the arrogance of power? Two years ago I published a book, *The Arrogance of American Power: What US Leaders Are Doing Wrong and Why It's Our Duty to Dissent*. At the time global public opinion against the United States was at its peak. The International Herald Tribune's John Freed reported on October 24, 2008 that Western European support for Obama had a lot to do with who the 44th president would be replacing. "While support for Barack Obama is broad and deep among Europeans, their reasons differ substantially from Americans who support him for president, according to a new survey. The survey, conducted by Harris Interactive for the IHT and the news channel France 24, reflects the overwhelming support in Western Europe for Obama, the Democratic presidential candidate, over John McCain, the Republican. And the main reason on both sides of the Atlantic is the same: Obama's capacity for change from the policies of President George W. Bush."

Those who study communication know very well that the magic bullet theory of direct communication from source to target is a dusty textbook anachronism. If what we intended others to receive were actually received, then we wouldn't be receiving such low marks in credibility. Not according to the myriad of global public opinion polls over the last four years.

In my 2006 critique of U.S. foreign policy (*The Arrogance of American Power*), I built a case that we were becoming seen as a one-hit wonder in international affairs—searching for a kind word for others to say about us or some small token of support for which we will heap out praise. Our public diplomacy reflected this search to be the world's American Idol. In the history of nations, we are a great power, often doing our duty as the "leader of the free world," but doesn't power when made so paramount give us a dizzying feeling. I, an American citizen, see no value in the U.S. being viewed as the Number One country in the world. Number One brings on so many challenges. And frankly it just doesn't hold.

The 21st Century is too important to leave in the hands of one nation-state. Whether we wish to halt global diseases, counter terrorism, weapons proliferation, fundamentalist thinking, or promote equitable development, economic enterprise, or the environment, we need to cooperate, even if we can't work out all our differences. I'll settle for Top 10. You can still make a good career out of it.

Despite my criticism of U.S. foreign policy, I do not wish to remove the U.S. government from the conduct of public diplomacy activities. A favorite J. William Fulbright axiom is this: "In a democracy, dissent is an act of faith. Like medicine, the test of its value is not in its taste but its effects." In other words, I believe that we need more broad-based and non-official executors of U.S. public diplomacy. We need those who can direct the terms of America's global engagements engagement in a more open dialogue with counterparts abroad and, through a multiplicity of voices, who can take a more active role in improving America's tarnished reputation.

To enable this, I'm hopeful that the new president will propose an *e pluribus unum*-style solution that draws on citizen diplomats and cultural mediators (those who are truly bicultural and bilingual) who can offer a full spectrum of attitudes about the American experience to prove that the United States can be diverse and unified at the same time. After the U.S. State Department so ceremoniously announced world figure skater Michelle Kwan as the country's new PD Ambassador in fall 2006, I started an Internet campaign to name Howard Zinn as the People's Ambassador. Professor Zinn said it was okay that I do that. I also urged that we have more sustained "track two" diplomacy, a process that is led by non-official actors and often over a long period of time to deal with deep-seated roots of international conflict. "Track two" does not replace "track one," or official diplomatic efforts. When Joseph Montville coined the term "track two diplomacy" in 1981, he wrote that it should "make its contribution as a supplement to the understandable shortcomings of official relations." I do think we need more of a shift from the efforts of government officials to those of ordinary citizens, but such efforts must be directive and purposive.

Let me make a final observation related to Track Two Diplomacy. Listen more, talk less. Remember, there's a two-to-one ratio between ears and mouth, something I need to keep reminding myself! We need to become more global, and not just in our material goods. Allen Goodman, President of the Institute for International Education, in early 2007 said the following:

> *For citizens of a global power, Americans are woefully uneducated about issues beyond our borders. The average adult American doesn't have a passport and can't locate France, let alone Iraq, on a map. Our TV networks devote less*

than five minutes a night to international news. Less than 1% of all Americans in college study abroad each year. Perhaps going to the movies can help. Movies today are a microcosm of our shrinking world, depicting global issues and taking viewers to far-flung locations.

In the age of Obama, will the world emerge smaller?

A NEW DEAL OR A HOUSE DIVIDED FOR AMERICAN PUBLIC DIPLOMACY?

If we're an arrogant nation, they'll resent us.

President George W. Bush

Long before he had two shoes hurtled at him at a news conference in Baghdad, President George W. Bush uttered that most visionary short statement about the state of the American brand and U.S. foreign policy at the turn of the century. It was during his second debate with Democratic presidential candidate Al Gore that Republican presidential nominee Bush cautioned our nation about its tendency to rub people the wrong way. He was also touting his style as a "compassionate conservative," which seemed to go well with the humility talk.

I know all about the former compassionate conservative. The one and only time I ever shook hands with our 43rd president was in summer 1999 when I attended a local ice cream stand in New Hampshire where then Governor Bush of Texas stopped by to hand out Compassionate Creamsicles. His security detail, the Texas Rangers, asked me to move aside because I just happened to be dressed as a chef with a large mixing bowl on which I wrote "Recipe for a Presidency: Lots and Lots of Dough." Did they think I was going to hurtle chocolate chip cookie dough toward the head of the next president? Oh, those lazy days of summer we once enjoyed before September 11, 2001.

After 9/11, President Bush said things like "smoke them out of their caves," "crusade," "War on Terror," "Axis of Evil," "Operation Shock and Awe" and ruined all that humble pie debate talk from October 2000.

Along comes 44, President-elect Barack Obama, whose style and grace as he lays claim to the highest office in the land makes true believers out of those of us who monitor Brand America. America, like my favorite football team, 'Bama, is back, big time.

We find it hard to believe that Obama will ever find himself in the situation that outgoing president Bush did as Muntadar al-Zaidi, a reporter for Al-Baghdadia TV, an independent satellite channel based in Cairo, said as he threw his shoes: "This is a gift from the Iraqis. This is the farewell kiss, you dog." After throwing the second shoe, al-Zaidi added: "This is from the widows, the orphans and those who were killed in Iraq." Bush quipped, "All I can report is it is a size 10."

The bottom of one's shoes is considered particularly dirty and distasteful in Islamic culture, which is why displaying the bottom of one's foot or shoe to someone else is considered disrespectful and an insult, almost the equivalent to the middle finger in the United States.

Publisher W. F. Zimmerman calls it "a classic cross-cultural insult, perceived as devastating by the thrower and an opportunity for a wisecrack by the recipient." The point of this shoe throwing insult to a foreign leader, an incident that may lead to at least two years' prison time, was to communicate in public (a new form of public diplomacy perhaps) what so many others would have wanted to say but were to afraid to act out. It was obviously distressing for the journalist to do what he did, and he has endured both ire and praise, depending on whom you ask, across the Middle East. What he seemed to be saying with his two throws was that after seven years of a Global War on Terror, Operation Shock and Awe, Axis of Evil, and righteous crusading, the US and its symbolic, though exiting leader, is no more part of the Arabic or Muslim community now than was Saddam or is Israel.

The ex-President Bush will continue on, to quote Zimmerman, "in magnificent imperviousness to outside opinion. I wonder if Obama ever saw anyone use a shoe for an insult when he was in Indonesia. The only way you can really appreciate the meaning of the insult is if you've lived in, absorbed, and to some degree bought into the cultural referents."

The shoe hurtling toward the American president is an ironic twist in the legacy of the man who promised to liberate the Iraqi people from the man his own father called the "new Hitler" of the Middle East. In 2003, a group of Iraqis was seen hitting a toppled statue of Saddam Hussein with their shoes in an obvious showing of ultimate disrespect for the deposed dictator. Though Bush may have evoked the ire of that international journalist and global public opinion in general, he is certainly no doppelgänger to Hussein. Nevertheless, the Bush approach of telling America's story to the world failed miserably and allowed Obama to secure the presidency with a recast of Senator John McCain as just a continuation of his Republican predecessor.

Barack Hussein Obama, who will use his full name at his swearing in as our next American president, will be in a position to, in his words, "reboot" American foreign policy and America's relationship with the Middle East in general, and the Arab Street (shorthand for public opinion) in particular. But how much can he accomplish against the backdrop of a domestic and global economy in free fall?

Will Obama be able to lay claim to a New Deal in public diplomacy as he is offering on the domestic economic front? If so, what will it look like? In style and rhetoric, Obama Soft Power will be a sharp contrast from the last three decades. He promised our nation and the world "change we can believe in," which, if it were any other candidate, would have been a laughable catch phrase for its anything but original flavor. Nevertheless, it stuck because Obama's personal narrative was truly different from any other presidential candidate we had seen. His message about New Foreign Policy is twofold: his administration will be "unyielding in stamping out terrorist extremism but also 'unrelenting in our desire to create a relationship of mutual respect and partnership with countries.'" This approach to crisis communication has disappointed many of Obama's left-leaning supporters who now accuse him of sounding too much like 43 and 42.

In foreign policy and national security where public diplomacy often lays its head at night, ultimately it is more likely that events and circumstances will drive change than personality, even though this president will likely become the most analyzed and written about "celebrity" (and yes, John McCain was right) in our history.

Shortly after the November 4th election I gave an interview to Al Jazeera English, which asked me about the bold changes Obama would lay out in his first 100 days. I told the news host that our next president was going to govern more from the middle as a pragmatic mediator rather than someone who would close down Guantanamo Bay on January 20, 2009. This seemed to disappoint my host, who reminded me how much affection the global community has for our new president. Wouldn't Obama want to move quickly on his promised changes? My answer: Not if he wants to survive those critical years in Washington where his opponents were already sharpening their proverbial knives in anticipation of a power shift.

Obama speaks very openly about his affection for a number of transformative and certainly bold presidents, not without notice several that grace Mount Rushmore. There is "16", Abraham Lincoln, about whom Obama told CBS's *60 Minutes* that "there is a wisdom there and a humility about his approach to government, even before he was president, that I just find helpful." We all recall Senator Obama's announcement of his presidential candidacy in front of the Old State House in Springfield, Illinois where his long ago predecessor once called upon a divided house to stand together. There is also Franklin Delano Roosevelt ("32"), whose Works Progress Administration inspires Obama's call for a nearly trillion-dollar economic stimulus plan to revive our economy. FDR, as we all know, wasn't able to keep his focus entirely at home. A Second World War with so much death and destruction is credited with helping America restart its economic engines as the domestic war front put so many back to work. We can all hope that this new president won't need such a historical event to jumpstart our crisis economy now.

BARACK HUSSEIN OBAMA

My Kennebunkport is on the South Side of Chicago.

President-elect Barack Hussein Obama

On January 20, 2009, the world will hear these words:

> *"I, Barack Hussein Obama, do solemnly swear that I will faithfully execute the office of President of the United States, and will to the best of my ability, preserve, protect and defend the Constitution of the United States."*

Obama will use his middle name, the name that was turned into a political football during the presidential campaign, as he takes the oath of office as leader of the free world and commander-in-chief of the armed forces of the United States, the man who is responsible for the nuclear football. This time as President that middle name might just come in handy in certain regions and religions.

I recall a dinner conversation I had with a group of Egyptian bloggers visiting Syracuse University in September 2008. They were here on a USAID grant to cover the presidential election. Sitting in Rachel's Restaurant at the downtown Sheraton just off campus, they asked me about my support for Obama, but more important, emphasized their support for him. "We view him as a Muslim like us," they declared, mainly because of his full name and his familial connection to Muslims, not only on his mother's side with her second marriage to a Muslim from Indonesia, but also his father's Muslim upbringing in Kenya. They found it incredible that the United States could possibly elect a man sympathetic to Muslims' plight, particularly their ongoing dispute with the state of Israel and against oppressive Muslim regimes in the Middle East.

I reminded them that Barack Obama was a self-proclaimed Christian and that these United States of America, though tolerant of all religions, had a Judeo-Christian heritage. In fact, it wasn't that long ago, forty-eight years to be precise, that another president had a tall task of winning over voters despite his Catholic upbringing.

Obama has been open about his Christian faith and practice. He left his home church, Chicago's Trinity United Church of Christ, after his former spiritual advisor Reverend Jeremiah Wright made remarks about 9/11 and became a campaign liability. Since then, Obama has said he set up a "sort of prayer circle across the country." These pastors from varied Christian denominations and other faiths agreed to pray for the president every morning on a conference call and sometimes Obama joined them on the call.

"I'm not even sure that all of them voted for me," he said. "But they were willing to pray for me, and that's something that was wonderful."[19]

If a plurality of Americans thought Obama were actually Muslim, his chances would be slim to none. This is not because of outright hatred from all Americans for Muslim believers. Haters abound, but they are not the majority of the electorate. Rather, it had much to do with perceived similarity. As a biracial candidate and Muslim, Obama risked being "too different" for the American electorate. As a Christian with a funny name whose face didn't look like those Founding Fathers we've come to know on our currency, Obama was more likely to win over voters' confidence and comfort in his being the 44th president of the United States.

Attitude change is predicated on basic principles. Likability is a major source for moving a needle positively in one's direction. Plain and simple, Obama was a likable candidate and exuded confidence without arrogance. He was more physically appealing and attractive than his Republican presidential opponent, John McCain. The 72-year-old McCain, who had won the 2000 New Hampshire Presidential Primary by 19 points over challenger George W. Bush,

---

[19] "Obama hopes to reboot US image among Muslims," Jennifer Loven, AP White House Correspondent, December 10, 2008.

was tagged as too old and out of touch 8 years later. He seemed even older and less attractive in contrast to his running mate. The Energizer Bunny-style Republican vice-presidential candidate Sarah Palin held her own in physical attractiveness. She was not running for president, however, and was quickly pilloried by both the real and fake news media for her empty, yet expensive, suit qualifications.

The next president laid out some lofty plans for using the global goodwill that has come his way to "recalibrate relations" in American foreign policy and international affairs. The Chicago Tribune reported, "Obama said the country must take advantage of a unique chance to recalibrate relations around the globe, through a new diplomacy that emphasizes inclusiveness and tolerance as well as an unflinching stand against terrorism."[20] As part of that reboot, Obama plans to give an address in an Islamic capital shortly after he takes office, a move sure to far exceed the favorability ratings that accrued to President George W. Bush when he visited the Islamic Center in Washington, D.C. shortly after the September 11, 2001 attacks.

Bush had violated the consistency principle that dominates textbooks in advertising and fundraising. Human beings generally prefer that politicians show consistency in principles, even if they don't always agree with them. When Bush said that the U.S. was on a "crusade" to "smoke out" the terrorist organizations and individuals behind the 9/11 attacks, he lumped together all Muslims in the world with those few who abuse the religion of Islam in support of their violent extremist ideologies. His visit to the Islamic Center was appreciated, but was also viewed as self-serving since he didn't change his rhetoric or behavior afterwards.

"I think we've got a unique opportunity to reboot America's image around the world and also in the Muslim world in

---

[20] As reported by the *Chicago Tribune*, December 9, 2008.

particular," Obama told a group of reporters from the *Chicago Tribune* on Tuesday, December 9, 2008, the first interview with a newspaper he granted since his historic election on November 4th. He promised an "unrelenting" desire to "create a relationship of mutual respect and partnership in countries and with peoples of good will who want their citizens and ours to prosper together."

The world, he said, "is ready for that message."

Maybe not everyone stateside, however. Featured reader comments in the *Minneapolis Star-Tribune* included these two:

> *Obama has clearly stated that he wants the US to become equal members of the world community. Watch as he shreds the oath of office (where he promises to uphold and defend the Constitution) for the sake of his global community. You can't be so tolerant that you sacrifice the best interests of the citizens of the United States. I'm afraid Obama is a world citizen first and secondly a US citizen. Global Village, 1—United States Constitution, 0. Be careful what change you vote for.*
>
> *Just why are we so obsessed with the world "loving" us? As long as we are the big dog we will be hated. As long as so many countries are dependent on us, we will be hated. As long as we stop oppression we will be hated. Even as we save the arses of countries, we will be hated. So what.*[21]

The persuader-in-chief believes that a sense of common purpose will overcome the deep scars left by racism in America. His bold new economic plan is designed to leap over a house divided. "The biggest challenges we face right now in improving race relations have to do with the universal concerns of Americans across color lines. If we are creating jobs throughout this economy, then African-Americans and Latinos, who are disproportionately unemployed, are going to be swept up in that rising tide."

---

[21] "Obama sees opportunity to reshape America's image," Christi Parsons, John McCormick, and Peter Nicholas, *Chicago Tribune*, December 9, 2008.

ALHURRA TV: UNCLE SAM'S BOONDOGGLE?

Figure 2. Edward R. Murrow

Given President Obama's promises to reboot American foreign policy, one wonders how far such a recalibration will take us. There are innumerable government boondoggles and the public diplomacy arena is no exception. One of the five pillars of public diplomacy is international broadcasting and the poster child of American government-sponsored broadcasting these days is Al Hurra (alternatively Alhurra) Television.

Nearly five years ago, I penned a column about the U.S. Government-sponsored 24-hour satellite broadcast television network. The title, "Al Hurra-Al Who?: Haven't heard? We're Free, They're Not!" illustrated my sense of alarm that taxpayers would be underwriting an operation that would be deemed discredited and cast off as so much American propaganda. The name alone for this station was enough of a problem. Here is my original essay from March 9, 2004:

Some three weeks ago the United States sent out a broadcast signal version of a Valentine's Day greeting card to win Arab hearts and minds. No Hallmark sentimentality like, "I'm thinking of you," but rather this greeting came in the form of a U.S. Government-funded Arabic language network with the very propagandistic moniker of "The Free One."

Al Hurra's free press mandate is to challenge what the U.S. Administration and the U.S. Broadcasting Board of Governors, which oversees international broadcasting perceive, as the hate media in the Arab region. In particular, Al Hurra offers a U.S. response to the barrage of anti-U.S. and anti-Israel stories and sensationalized imagery coming from the more popular networks of Al-Jazeera and Al-Arabiya.

President Bush says that Al Hurra will help combat "the hateful propaganda that fills the airwaves in the Muslim world and tell people the truth about the values and policies of the United States." It seems to be doing so from a safe distance. Al Hurra is based, not in the Middle East, but in northern Virginia, U.S.A.

While you might think that eyeballs would be glued to the U.S.-declared truthful alternative, so far no one is fully embracing the "free one" version, despite financing of $62 million in congressional funding for the first year alone.

A quick review of some of the global media reaction spells trouble for Al Hurra. Arab newspaper editorials have been universally thumbs down on the new broadcast alternative, with the not unexpected negative reaction of "it's all American propaganda, anyway." The Cairo Times said that many Egyptians remain "guarded" in their reaction and are suspicious of the new station's propagandistic potential to shape news from a pro-U.S., pro-Israeli governmental perspective. The most prestigious Arabic-language newspaper, Al Ahram, said "It is difficult to understand how the U.S., with its advanced research centers and clever minds, explains away Arab hatred as a product of a demagogic media and not due to its biased policies and propensity to abuse Arab interests."

Arab News, the Middle East's leading English daily, reports a "cool reception" to Al Hurra, which some viewers see as "short on credibility and long on arrogance." Ouch! Not the long and the short of it you want.

The former minister of information in Kuwait, Dr. Saad Al Ajmi, reports a mixed review. In a special to the Gulf News, he says, "there is most certainly a vacuum for it [Al Hurra] to fill. Before Al Hurra, America had no satellite television voice in the Arab world......Al Hurra is playing catch up, and it remains to be seen if it will be successful."

CNN did dominate the Arab airwaves in the early 1990s but this was during the last war in the Gulf and before Al Jazeera and Al Arabiya came along to challenge this English-language global media station that was accessible to only English-speaking elites in the region.

What remains to be seen is if those who initially condemn the network will find curiosity getting the best of them and sneak a peek, if nothing else, to see if Al Hurra offers anything new and different in both content and production value.

Against a backdrop of anti-Americanism and an unfinished roadmap to peace in the Middle East, it's doubtful that many hearts and minds will be won for now. The U.S. just doesn't have the freedom credibility it wants to project to the Middle East. Just calling a network free doesn't make it so, especially one tied so closely to the U.S. government.

Telling to some Arab viewers was that President Bush was the first guest interviewed on Al Hurra. Al-Quds Al-Arabi, a newspaper generally critical of the U.S., said that the Bush interview "brought to mind official channels broadcast by

> *regimes mired in dictatorship, just like those of the 1960s and beginning of the '70s."*
>
> *The greatest hurdle to overcome seems to be in the naming of the station itself. To many, if Al Hurra represents "the free ones" then that makes "us" the unfree ones. This magic bullet theory of communication assumes that the sender's need for more free speech and more accurate information about itself in a region coincides with the receiver's needs. But many naysayers to Al Hurra say that the U.S. still "just doesn't get it" about what the Arab audience true needs are.*
>
> *One magazine writer, Amy Moufai, told an NBC News producer in Cairo that she hadn't watched the new U.S. network, but was "very surprised they would choose a name like that which highlights the fact they don't know what they are doing in the Middle East. It reeks of the whole notion of a white man's bread. 'Let us teach you our free ways.'"*
>
> *The United States, "the big one," tends to associate better communication with more information. If we can just get our message out there, make it louder, make it stronger, make it bolder, then we'll be well on our way to repairing miscommunication problems. But just maybe what is sought is more respectability and acknowledgment that U.S. geopolitical and economic interests in the region don't often match up to how the Arab people perceive freedom, particularly from despotic government intervention.*
>
> *A government-led free press is a harsh reminder of a region dominated by unfree governments. And no slick slogans or pretty newsroom sets are going to overcome those realities.*

Two years after that article, the *Los Angeles Times* published an op-ed piece, "The Limits of Propaganda," by Anatol Lieven and David Chambers that was even stronger in its language:

> *One of the chief means by which democracy was supposed to be preached to Arabs is the U.S. Arabic-*

> *language television station Al Hurra ("the Free One") and its sister station, Radio Sawa ("Together"). Instead, these government-funded stations represent everything that is wrong and misconceived about official U.S. ways of approaching the Arab world. Widespread Muslim fury at the European media's caricatures of the prophet Muhammad, and widespread Western incomprehension of that fury, illustrate the extent to which we are still talking past each other. Clearly there is an urgent need for media that will bridge this gap. But to be effective, they have to be credible with Muslims – which Al Hurra is not.*[22]

Al Hurra lacks credibility because it is modeled on the propaganda media of the Cold War like Radio Liberty and Radio Free Europe. These media targeted citizens who sought total liberation from their oppressive, dictatorial regimes. But the Arab Middle East is a different region. Though its regimes are oppressive, its inhabitants wish to reform and modernize regimes and reject efforts by the U.S. to underwrite corrupt governments. Al Hurra also assumes that the Arab world is without access to diverse media. There now exist over 200 satellite television channels in the Middle East. Al Jazeera and Al Arabiya TV dominate the news, but upstart media channels are proliferating not only on traditional media but also through the efforts of young bloggers (like the USAID-funded bloggers I met on the Syracuse University campus) who are challenging the status quo. Lieven and Chambers pull no punches regarding Al Hurra and its anachronistic status:

> *The propaganda techniques of the Cold War made sense once. But such state propaganda is not the real American way. Rather, our approach should be based on Oliver Wendell Holmes' belief that "the best test of truth is the power of the thought to get itself accepted in the competition of the market." The Arab media provide such a market. Let's*

---

[22] Anatol Lieven and David Chambers, "The limits of propaganda," Los Angeles Times, February 13, 2006, B-13.

compete in it with the high-quality, independent media that the U.S. produces and Arabs respect. Al Hurra should be closed down at once.[23]

Well that was then, this is then too.

On December 10, 2008, the Bush Administration released a fact sheet illustrating its strong support for global human rights. "Today, President Bush will commemorate Human Rights Day and the 60th anniversary of the adoption of the Universal Declaration of Human Rights by the United Nations General Assembly in 1948. To honor the day, President Bush is meeting with activists who use Internet blogs and new-media technologies to promote freedom in countries with restricted media environments—six in person and two via videoconference—including individuals from Belarus, Burma, China, Cuba, Egypt, Iran, and Venezuela. President Bush will discuss with them the challenges they confront in overcoming censorship."

One of the administration's noteworthy human rights accomplishments was BBG-sponsored international broadcasting efforts, including Al Hurra Television. The BBG consists of a bipartisan board of presidentially-appointed members that oversees all government-sponsored international broadcasting, including the Voice of America (VOA), Radio Free Europe/Radio Liberty (RFE/RL), Radio Free Asia (RFA), Radio and TV Martí, and the Middle East Broadcasting Networks (MBN)—Radio Sawa and Al Hurra Television. Here is what the White House fact sheet disclosed about the BBG and its Human Rights Focus:

Defending The Rights Of Independent Journalists And New-Media Users Fighting For Freedom Across The Globe

The Administration has helped users of new media to overcome censorship, report abuses, and advocate for freedom. U.S. international broadcasters funded by the

---

[23] Ibid.

Broadcasting Board of Governors (BBG) are overcoming censorship by gathering news from citizen journalists with cell phones, reporting the facts via SMS feeds and targeted e-mails, and encouraging citizens living in repressive regimes to join the information revolution with open discussions on radio and TV call-in shows and blogs. The BBG now offers diverse Internet products in all 60 broadcast languages, ranging from basic text to complex video and audio and live streaming.

The BBG works with a network of non-governmental organizations to develop anti-web-censorship software and technical tools. These media freedom tools are available free of charge in English, Farsi, Kazakh, Mandarin, and Vietnamese at the websites of BBG's language services which are accessible through www.bbg.gov. The Administration has increased funding for the BBG from $441 million in FY 2001 to more than $670 million in FY 2008. BBG's commitment to using new media to defend freedom of expression has helped increase the combined audience for all its broadcasts from 100 million to more than 175 million weekly since September 11, 2001.[24]

On December 11, 2008, the Broadcasting Board of Governors (BBG) released a cascade of candor (to paraphrase David Frost's hoped for outcome with Richard Nixon) about the effectiveness and audience reach of Al Hurra Television. The candor came in the form of three 2008 studies of the broadcast network, two from academic institutions (University of Southern California, University of Missouri) and one from the State Department's own Office of the Inspector General. One study emerged as Mighty Mouse, completed by my colleagues in the Center on Public Diplomacy at the Annenberg School, University of Southern California.

---

[24] The White House: Office of the Press Secretary, December 10, 2008. "Fact Sheet: Promoting Human Rights Worldwide."

This mousetrap led to temporary blindness for the Broadcasting Board of Governors that oversees Al Hurra TV. The BBG chose to sit on the USC report for over four months, despite the report's completion on July 31, 2008 and before the November presidential election, as it attempted to work out some appropriate public relations campaign that would minimize the damage.

The station's name, Al Hurra, continues to violate the similarity principle in creating liking and influencing individuals. The principle is simple. The more similar a source and its audience, the more the audience will move in concert with a source's objectives. The more dissimilar the source and its audience, the more the audience will move away from the source's goal of positive attitude change. This is why we see far more "average looking" people in TV commercial testimonials. They look more like the viewers watching.

If the U.S. is deemed the "Free One," that automatically assumes that its audience is unfree, and by definition, inferior. Further, is it really rational for a government that is often criticized for its policies in the Middle East to sponsor its own self-described free and independent media. How free can such a media be?

Larry Register, a former CNN executive with 20 years' experience, was in charge of Al Hurra for about 18 months until he allowed some highly critical opponents of the U.S. and Israel to air their views on the government network. Register said that allowing such opinion was designed to help build more credibility for the network in a region already highly suspicious of government-sponsored anything.

More credibility means, "Not just picking and choosing what you might want to cover because it's favorable for your side versus their side. Cover all of it. Tell the whole story. Part of the idea is Al Hurra is the free one. The name is 'The Free One.'" Register learned that the U.S. Government respected free speech on Al Hurra as long as it was in keeping with U.S. policy in the region. Airing a speech by

Nasrallah, the head of Hezbollah, was one of the reasons Register had to resign his position as head of Al Hurra.

The following is a lengthy but important executive summary of USC's 72-page study for the BBG. The study began in September 2007 and was turned in to the BBG in July 2008. It was held back for public distribution by the BBG for over four months but finally released on December 11, 2008.

> *Primary Conclusions:*
>
> *A lack of news and topical programming tailored to the interests of the Arab audience: Our study found that Al Hurra's programming was perceived as being similar to traditional, state-funded broadcasting in the region. Not only has Al Hurra done little to distinguish itself from second-tier Middle Eastern broadcasters in terms of its news agenda, but it has also failed to develop the distinctive style, format, and breadth of coverage that might attract a substantial audience. Even Al Hurra's reporting of U.S. policies and American life is seen by Arab viewers as undistinguished. This opinion ran through the discussion group sessions and was supported by the content analysis. In short, Al Hurra has failed to become competitive.*
>
> *Weak Journalism: The quality of Al Hurra's journalism is substandard on several levels. Its technical presentation is not as proficient as that of the best Arab channels. The study's content analysis found that Al Hurra's news stories lack appropriate balance and sourcing. Discussion group respondents noted journalists' apparent lack of experience and flawed presentation of news, including the poor use of graphics and a lack of standardized Arabic language. The content analysis found that Al Hurra relied on unsubstantiated information too often, allowed the on-air expression of personal judgments too frequently, and failed to present opposing views in over 60 percent of its news stories.*
>
> *Perceived bias: Given Al Hurra's association with the U.S. government and polices, there exists a natural skepticism*

among Arab audiences regarding the broadcaster's ability to report objectively about issues in the region. Our content analysis found several factors that could further such impressions of bias, including:

1. Al Hurra's news was likely to promote Western perspectives at the expense of Arab perspectives. When Al Hurra was critical of a particular view of issues, it was six times more likely to be critical of the Arab/other perspective than the Western viewpoint. Moreover, it was twice as likely to praise the Western outlook rather than the Arab/other perspective.

2. When personal judgments were expressed, they were likely to be pro-West or anti-Arab. Rarely were opinions expressed that were critical of a Western perspective or supportive of an Arab position, particularly on such sensitive topics as the Israeli-Arab conflict and Arab human rights issues.

3. The use of unsubstantiated information was often associated with a bias in favor of Western perspectives and U.S. policy. Reporting that was grounded in unsubstantiated information (which includes over 12 percent of Al Hurra's news content) was twice as likely to favor the Western viewpoint over the Arab/other perspective, and almost three times less likely to be critical of U.S. policy.

4. Al Hurra was much more critical of Arab governments and political opposition groups than it was of U.S. policy in the region. Reporting was twice as critical of Arab political positions and policies as it was of U.S. policies.

5. Seen as Propaganda: Discussion group participants felt that Al Hurra's reporting, when stacked against its competitors in the region, represented a false or tilted perspective of events, especially with regard to its coverage of Iraq and the Israeli-Arab conflict. Discussion group members also felt that Al Hurra's news was overly critical of Arab political and opinion leaders. It is important to note that, while the U.S. policy and viewpoints were often clearly identified, participants thought that they were unpersuasive or included too little explanation. While some identified Al Hurra's coverage as being more positive with regard to the possibilities of peace and stability in the region, these attributes were more often seen as evidence of an agenda rather than coverage that provoked a different point of view.

6. A Lack of Connection to the "Arab street": Discussion group participants felt that Al Hurra too often relied on official sources about issues important to the general Arab public. Rarely were sources entirely independent, and the voice of the average Arab was either non-existent or subordinated to official pronouncements. Moreover, coverage of highly divisive issues—Israeli-Arab conflict and Iraq in particular—was often seen as overly optimistic with regard to the possibilities of stability and reconciliation. Further, the paucity of coverage of Islam and Islamic-related issues indicates insensitivity to one of the fundamental elements of most Arabs' lives.

My own conclusions: Al Hurra has never produced a large audience share and has not built up a credible broadcast profile in the target publics of the Middle East. There is no evidence that Al Hurra's existence has kept the American public any safer or served a substantive public information service function in the Middle East. The public's trust that government avoid waste, fraud and abuse in taxpayer-funded programs has been violated. It shouldn't take hundreds of thousands in government-sponsored studies to come to those conclusions. I blogged about this on the Huffington Post for free!

Having said that, my criticism of Al Hurra is given with the full knowledge that Al Hurra may very well continue under the Obama-Biden administration. Washington is all about power-brokering, and unless Al Hurra gets immersed in some major scandal, it is likely to continue operation, though I hope with some much-needed reforms.

Both the University of Southern California's Annenberg School for Communication and the University of Missouri's School of Journalism are commissioned studies designed to enhance the credibility of this government operation. USC's study, which was based on a whole month's content analysis of Al Hurra programming, was much more critical in its conclusions and undoubtedly earned the ire of many within the BBG and State Department. The University of Missouri report, for which there is just a short focus group report available, was much more in alignment with BBG's own conclusions about Al Hurra.

The University of Missouri report was prominently highlighted in a BBG press release, with a pull quote that read, "Despite recent criticism in the American media and politically biased criticism in the Middle East, Al Hurra Television does most things right most of the time. This is born out by critical review of Al Hurra news stories and newscasts." The Missouri focus group project focused on journalism best practices and assumed the legitimacy of Al Hurra:

> *"For the most part, Al Hurra journalists are conditioned to a very different kind of journalism. They were trained to report the stories of the totalitarian governments that owned and operated the media. They were, in fact, propagandists for the messages of the government. Their journalism-of-origin is nothing like the journalism culture of independence and public service in American and most Western countries."*
>
> *"Al Hurra, thus, has a competitive opportunity unlike any other television operation serving the Middle East. If Al Hurra can transition its correspondents, videographers, editors and producers into the American tradition (as best described as the 'elements of journalism'), then Al Hurra will have a significant competitive advantage over Al Jazeera, Al Arabiya and the many other television news operations in the region."*
>
> *The Elements of Journalism include:*
>
> - *Journalism's first obligation is to the truth.*
> - *Its loyalty is to the citizens.*

• Its discipline is that of verification.

• Journalism must be independent from sources.

• It must serve – at times – as a watchdog.

• Journalism should serve as a public forum for ideas and criticism.

• It must be relevant and interesting (i.e., incorporate best practices of storytelling).

• Journalism must be comprehensive and proportional.

(From the book The Elements of Journalism by Kovach and Rosenstiel.)

"Al Hurra Television's fast-track development is unrivaled in American television history. Never before has so much been done so fast: Funding the operation,

establishing operations centers in the U.S. and in the Middle East, hiring personnel (difficult-to-recruit key personnel being Arabic speakers with significant journalism credentials) securing vendors of complicated technologies and creating systems and policies. This has been a daunting task, well managed to this point – despite the need for more editorial control."

"Clearly, journalism everywhere is subject to criticism and second-guessing and political influence. Compare the current critique of the American media in the coverage of the domestic presidential campaign to the more complicated political ,ethnic, religious and nationalistic environment in which Al Hurra operates.

That said, Al Hurra Television must now take two big steps: radically improve editorial control to eliminate bias and imbalance in coverage, and teach staff the best practices in television news storytelling and production."

The clearest read on the Al Hurra controversy doesn't emerge from the puffy pages of the Missouri report that touts the idealized elements of journalism. Rather, it comes from the salaried efforts of former *Washington Post* national reporter, Dafna Linzer. Linzer, whom I interviewed for this chapter, said that when she was working as a national security writer at the *Post,* she kept being told by her sources to investigate what was going on at Al Hurra. It wasn't until she was hired by the independent investigative nonprofit ProPublica organization in winter 2008 that she was able to pitch the story idea to her senior editors. Linzer's ProPublica resume reads as follows:

> *Dafna Linzer has been a national security reporter for* The Washington Post, *covering intelligence and nonproliferation, since 2004. Her coverage of the Iranian nuclear issue won the United Nations 2005 Gold Medal award for international reporting. Before joining the Post, she spent ten years as a foreign correspondent for Associated Press. Based in Jerusalem, New York, and the United Nations, she reported from more than a dozen countries covering terrorism, nonproliferation, and conflict. Her reporting from Baghdad, on the hunt for weapons of mass destruction, won national attention and praise, ending with her report that the fruitless hunt had quietly come to an end.*

There is nothing in that resume of ProPublica's senior reporter that suggests someone who is out to get Al Hurra. Rather, Linzer's mission at ProPublica is to investigate the stories that the major corporate media are no longer doing due to newsroom personnel cutbacks or don't wish to do altogether. As much as I admire the elements of journalism as outlined by Kovach and Rosenstiel,[25] the real world of journalism today is a newsroom bereft of resources to support investigative reporters who wish to work on stories and dig for sources and story angles over many months.[26] ProPublica is designed to fill in that gap.

---

[25] "What is Journalism For," by Bill Kovach and Tom Rosenstiel, Poynter Online, October 13, 2006;
http://www.poynter.org/dg.lts/id.4973/content.content_view.htm
[26] "Today's investigative reporters lack resources," Special to the *Arizona Republic* by

Linzer got cracking on the Al Hurra story shortly after her hiring and by June 2008, her investigative stories of Al Hurra lead to a 13-minute report conducted by CBS News' "60 Minutes." A highly respected professor at the University of Maryland, Dr. Shibley Telhami, was asked about Al Hurra's effectiveness. Shibley told Scott Pelley of 60 Mintues, "I think by and large it's irrelevant." Telhami has conducted Arab public opinion polls in the Middle East for the last six years. The most popular channel that the Bush Administration has hated since 2001 remains Al Jazeera, which holds over 50 percent of the Arab audience. Al Hurra, in contrast, ranks at the bottom of viewership. "I think in there, it takes about two percent." "So, after half a billion dollars spent on Al Hurra, the effect in the region has been what?" Pelley asks. "In terms of public opinion, less than zero," Telhami says.

Telhami told 60 Minutes what so many of us who study public opinion and foreign policy have been saying for years. The so-called Arab Street (public opinion in the Middle East) is disdainful of U.S. policies in the region. Says Telhami, it's not what we say, but what we do that hurts the most. "It's what we do in Iraq. It's what we do on the Arab-Israeli issue. It's how we define our war on terrorism. Most people interpret it as a war on Islam. Every single year, anger with America has increased. Think about how could you get to that point if you're succeeding?"

The Bush Administration was always quick to point out that Al Hurra's largest audience is in Iraq, where Telhami does not conduct public opinion polling. Undersecretary of State for Public Diplomacy James Glassman says that up to 26 million Iraqis per week tune in to part of Al Hurra Television programming, including a popular cultural program on the rise in popularity of wearing fashionable blue jeans in the Middle East. Glassman disputed Telhami's conclusions. "We're not irrelevant. We're doing things

---

Chelsea Ide and Kanupriya Vashisht, May 28, 2006;
http://www.azcentral.com/specials/special01/0528bolles-stateofreporting.html

that other broadcasters are not doing. We're doing thorough coverage, for example, of the elections in Morocco. We're talking about what's really going on in Egypt. We're talking about what's happening with women in the Middle East."

Director of Communications for the Middle East Broadcasting Networks (MBN) Deirdre Kline attacked Linzer for her "repeated errors and distortions" in several articles and said that they "do not live up to ProPublica's Code of Ethics." A 15-page memo accompanied the letter to Paul Steiger, ProPublica's Editor-in-Chief.[27] Undeterred, Linzer continued to ask the BBG for copies of Al Hurra studies and was the first reporter to reveal that the BBG had finally paid USC for its study (estimated at nearly $200,000) while the University of Missouri School of Journalism had received a grant to conduct journalism training for Al Hurra reporters. Altogether, Al Hurra has a budget of $500,000 to do journalism training, a small portion of which is allocated to Missouri. [28]

In November 2008 I traveled to Southern California to give several talks, including a panel discussion on public diplomacy sponsored by the USC Center on Public Diplomacy at the Annenberg School for Communication. While in town, I visited briefly with Dean Ernest J. Wilson III, "Ernie" to most of us, who was appointed Dean of the Annenberg School for Communication in spring 2008. Ernie asked if I had access to any public diplomacy briefing papers for the Obama-Biden Transition Team. Within a few days, I understood the request. Ernie Wilson was named to the transition team overseeing public diplomacy for President-elect Obama. Ernie is the right choice for an administration emphasizing

---

[27] See a complete list of Al Hurra resources here:
http://www.propublica.org/feature/alhurra-resources

[28] Dafna Linzer, "Report Calls Alhurra a Failure," ProPublica.org, December 11, 2008; http://www.propublica.org/article/report-calls-alhurra-a-failure-1211. See also "Mad TV
U.S. taxpayers subsidize terrorist propaganda and Holocaust denial in the Arab world," by Joel Mowbray, *Wall Street Journal* Op-Ed, May 1, 2007.

change in foreign policy. He knows Washington insider politics but also seems capable of maintaining an objective stance with a strong orientation toward the public interest and public service needed to assess public diplomacy issues in general and international broadcasting in particular.

Though Ernie Wilson didn't ask my opinion directly, I share this advice about government-sponsored public diplomacy free of charge: In everything related to taxpaper monies (mine, his, and theirs) the first goal should be to streamline programs and cut the fat, including those programs like Al Hurra and Radio/TV Marti (a Reagan hangover) that show evidence of politically-charged maneuvering to sustain them. In 1998, I published my first book on public diplomacy, *Propaganda, Inc.*, reissued in a second edition in 2002. In it, I argued that Radio/TV Marti was much maligned, and the then United States Information Agency sponsored Office of Cuba Broadcasting was overly politicized with supporters of the Cuban-American National Foundation and its controversial founder, Jorge Mas Canosa, who chaired USIA's Advisory Board for Cuba Broadcasting, and who was accused by at least one anti-Castro activist Luis Posada of supporting clandestine terrorist activities to overthrow Castro's Communist government.[29]

Canosa was able to use his bullying charisma and his organization's clout to secure millions of dollars from the Reagan, Bush, and Clinton administrations in annual funding for Radio Marti and its TV cousin, despite internal reports that acknowledged TV Marti "achieves virtually no reception or impact within the greater Havana area due to heavy jamming."[30] Wayne Smith of the Center for International Policy in Washington, D.C. (and former chief of the U.S. Interests Section in Havana) revealed in 1997 that

---

[29] "Posada: 'I'll kill Castro if it's the last thing I do,'" Edward Helmore in Miami, *London Observer*, July 19, 1998; http://www.hartford-hwp.com/archives/43b/146.html.
[30] As reported in *Broadcasting and Cable* magazine, March 21, 1994, p. 61.

TV Marti's signal, which was coming from a balloon high above the Florida Keys, used the same transmission signal that the U.S. Government was using to track incoming drug flights. When TV Marti's signal went on, the drug smuggling radar went off.[31]

The evidence seems clear that Radio/TV Marti, like Al Hurra TV, are respectively Cold War and War on Terror weapons, controlled by powerful vested interests resistant to transparency in government objectives and public interest scrutiny. A recent example of this intransigence follows. When I posted a column, "Must Read About Al Hurra TV" on December 14, 2008, I received a critical post from a Letitia King, who challenged my statement that the University of Missouri School of Journalism had received a $500,000 contract to conduct training of Al Hurra journalists. She wrote: "Want to be sure you have the facts straight. The allegation that the University of Missouri was granted a $500,000 contract is totally false. Appreciate you making a correction." I immediately called Dafna Linzer at ProPublica to verify my facts and to check about Ms. King's qualifications. Linzer said that Letitia King was the official spokesperson for the Broadcasting Board of Governors, though King herself failed to identify this organizational identification in her post on my Web page. Her official title is Acting Director, Office of Public Affairs, Broadcasting Board of Governors.[32] (I did correct my post—that Missouri is receiving just a small part of the $500,000 in journalism training. In the process, I found out that Letitia and I had served as Presidential Management Fellows at the U.S. Information Agency. Small world, isn't it?)

---

[31] Wayne S. Smith, "Pirating Radio Marti," *The Nation*, January 27, 1997. See also Peter Kornbluth and Jon Elliston, "Pricey, Stupid, and Wrong: Will Congress Kill TV Marti?," *The Nation*, August 22/29, 1994.

[32] See Press Release, "Letter to the Public Diplomacy Council from the Broadcasting Board of Governors' Spokesperson," Letitia M. King, November 24, 2008, Washington, D.C., http://www.bbg.gov/pressroom/pressreleases-article.cfm?articleID=330.

While I'm willing to give anyone, including government spokespersons, the benefit of the doubt, I wonder why the Broadcasting Board of Governors is so defensive. If Al Hurra TV really is a legitimate news source in the Middle East, then I'm one U.S. citizen who supports it. I'm already a strong advocate for Voice of America. I just have not seen any evidence that Al Hurra TV is pulling its weight alongside existing Middle East media sources like Al Arabiya TV, Al Jazeera or even BBC Radio. As of this writing, I've been extended an invitation from Letitia King to visit the BBG and Al Hurra in order to demonstrate that it is an effective tool in the public diplomacy arsenal. I look forward to reporting back on my findings.

THE NIXON INTERVIEWS WITH DAVID FROST:

A CLASSIC STUDY OF THE PRESS/POLITICS POWER STRUGGLE WITH LESSONS FOR OBAMA

[The antiwar movement is] a wild orgasm of anarchists sweeping across the country like a prairie fire.

--Richard M. Nixon

Figure 3. Richard M. Nixon

.1977 was an eventful year in American popular culture. I bought one of my first albums, the Bee Gees' "Saturday Night Fever" movie soundtrack, and watched John Travolta bump and grind in that white tuxedo along with millions of other curious young teenage girls across America. Another classic album that every American household seemed to own was Fleetwood Mac's "Rumours" album. I recall playing Ping-Pong with my brother in the basement of our family home in Greenville, South Carolina with "Rhiannon" floating out like cotton candy through the speakers. I was attending Bob Jones Academy, a fundamentalist Christian school on the campus of Bob Jones University. Bob Jones would not have been happy with my choice of albums.

The New York celebrity-drenched cocaine-stained discothèque, Studio 54, opened on April 26, 1977 where Disco queen Donna Summer's "I Feel Love" became a gold standard. It remains to this day one of the most sampled songs of all time. Take a listen.

Against that backdrop and not feeling the love that year was disgraced president, Richard Milhouse Nixon. Holed up in his seaside villa, La Casa Pacifica at San Clemente, Nixon was contacted by David Frost for a series of four televised interviews. The price tag was $600,000 in exchange for the exclusive, including one televised interview devoted exclusively to Watergate. On one side sat David Frost, who was hoping to add some gravitas to his reputation in television journalism by eliciting something like a confession or at least contrition connected to the Watergate scandal that drove Nixon from office three years earlier. On the other side sat a former commander-in-chief and CEO of America, Inc. who desired a rehabilitation of his place and standing in the world. Both men had much to gain and everything to lose from this showdown. Nixon calculated that Frost would be an easy mark.

The interviews, which first aired in May 1977, were stunning for the day, likely never to be repeated. Just ask yourself, who would be the David Frost to a George W. Bush or Barack Obama? Katie Couric? Charlie Gibson? The Nixon interview with David Frost drew the largest global TV audience for a news interview in recorded history. In the United States alone, 45 million people watched, an extraordinary number given the estimated population then of 220 million (compared to today's 305 million). The interviews were conducted over 28 hours, with two full days devoted just to Watergate.

Ron Howard's "Frost/Nixon" takes a psychic close-up of the heavyweight politician Nixon and his likely lightweight challenger, the talk show host David Frost. It has been described as "the ultimate face-off in the court of public opinion," a precursor to all the confessional talk show formats of today.

NIXON: And I shall be your fiercest adversary. I shall come at you with everything I got. Because the limelight can only shine on one of us. And for the other, it'll be the wilderness...with nothing, and no one for company but those voices ringing in our head.

FROST: Except that only one of us can win.

The film's production notes reveal what such an interview did to the public's collective consciousness on politics and journalism: "Their legendary confrontation would revolutionize the art of the confessional interview, change the face of politics and capture an admission from the former president that startled people all over the world... possibly even including Nixon himself. Nixon surprised everyone by selecting Frost as his televised confessor, intending to easily outfox the breezy British showman and reclaim his status as a supreme statesman in the hearts and minds of Americans. Likewise, Frost's team harbored doubts about his ability to hold his own against Nixon. As cameras rolled, a charged battle of wits ensued. Would Nixon evade questions of his role in one of the nation's greatest disgraces? Or would Frost confound critics and bravely demand accountability from the most skilled politician of his generation? The encounter would reveal each man's insecurities, ego and reserves of dignity—as both ultimately set aside posturing in a stunning display of unvarnished truth."

Despite the popular sentiment that a British jet-setting playboy personality like Frost could not match the political wile of the American president, Frost managed to pull out a revealing confession of sorts from Nixon, namely that the president is above the law on issues of national security. As recorded by the New York Times, here is a memorable exchange during the Watergate interview segment:

FROST: Pulling some of our discussions together, as it were; speaking of the Presidency and in an interrogatory filed with the Church Committee, you stated, quote, "It's quite obvious that there are certain inherently government activities, which, if undertaken by the sovereign in protection of the interests of the nation's security are lawful, but which if undertaken by private persons, are not." What, at root, did you have in mind there?

NIXON: Well, what I, at root I had in mind I think was perhaps much better stated by Lincoln during the War Between the States. Lincoln said, and I think I can remember the quote almost exactly, he said, "Actions which otherwise would be unconstitutional, could become lawful if undertaken for the purpose of preserving the Constitution and the Nation."

Now that's the kind of action I'm referring to. Of course in Lincoln's case it was the survival of the Union in wartime, it's the defense of the nation and, who knows, perhaps the survival of the nation.

FROST: But there was no comparison was there, between the situation you faced and the situation Lincoln faced, for instance?

NIXON: This nation was torn apart in an ideological way by the war in Vietnam, as much as the Civil War tore apart the nation when Lincoln was president. Now it's true that we didn't have the North and the South—

FROST: But when you said, as you said when we were talking about the Huston Plan, you know, "If the president orders it, that makes it legal," as it were: Is the president in that sense—is there anything in the Constitution or the Bill of Rights that suggests the president is that far of a sovereign, that far above the law?

NIXON: No, there isn't. There's nothing specific that the Constitution contemplates in that respect. I haven't read every word, every jot and every title, but I do know this: That it has been, however, argued that as far as a president is concerned, that in war time, a president does have certain extraordinary powers which would make acts that would otherwise be unlawful, lawful if undertaken for the purpose of

> *preserving the nation and the Constitution, which is essential for the rights we're all talking about.*[33]

Nixon would never again confront the subject of Watergate so directly. The rules of the interview were strict: (1) No advance screening of questions and (2) No right to see, much less, revise the program before broadcast.

Richard Nixon, the thirty-seventh president of the United States, died on April 22, 1994 at age 81, after successfully releasing ten bestselling books and redefining himself as an elder statesman in international affairs. Sir David Frost, now 69, is hosting *Frost Over the World*, a weekly television interview and news talk program syndicated on Al Jazeera English. Watch this revealing interview by David Frost with Benazir Bhutto, just a little over a month before her murder (http://www.youtube.com/watch?v=oIO8B6fpFSQ).

We can only hope that the 44th president of the United States will not have to sit down for any press interview that requires his explanation of unlawful actions in the service of the national interest.

---

[33] From the third Nixon-Frost interview, *The New York Times*, May 20, 1977, p. A16.

WINNING THE WAR OF IDEAS IN THE AGE OF OBAMA

Our priority is not to promote our brand but to help destroy theirs.

James Glassman, Undersecretary of State for Public Diplomacy

In July 2008, the new Undersecretary of State for Public Diplomacy and Public Affairs James Glassman gave his first speech entitled "Winning the War of Ideas" at The Washington Institute for Near East Policy (WINEP). Glassman is fond of saying that "a war of ideas is at least as important as military action." He follows many government officials before him like Vice President Joe Biden who said after 9/11 "No matter how powerful our military is, we will not be powerful if we lose the war of ideas."[34] Former Secretary of Defense Donald Rumsfeld was, like Glassman, a devotee of the military approach to corralling the public will. Rumsfeld once said that the U.S. was losing the war of ideas.[35] "Our enemies have skillfully adapted to fighting wars in today's media age, but ... our country has not adapted. For the most part, the U.S. government still functions as a 'five and dime' store in an eBay world."[36]

Most of us open source folks who believe that sunshine is the best disinfectant are not fond of the term "war of ideas," though Glassman readily acknowledges that there is no good substitute, save soft power or smart power. The reason we don't like the phrase is that it reminds us of our recent troubled past, the GWOT (Global War on Terror), Long War, GSAVE (Global Struggle Against Violent Extremism) Bush-Cheney era that followed 9/11. All of these

---

[34] Ira Teinowitz, "Congress will support the war of ideas," *Advertising Age*, June 17, 2002.
[35] Bill Gertz, "Rumsfeld pushes 'new sense of urgency'; 'War of ideas' needed to defeat the terrorists," *The Washington Times*, October 24, 2003.
[36] "New Realities in the Media Age: A Conversation with Donald Rumsfeld," Council on Foreign Relations, February 17, 2006.

monikers inflamed negative attitudes toward the U.S. since they were viewed as tied primarily to U.S. national security interests and not global security concerns.

A war of ideas approach isolates our thinking into perpetuating an adversarial Cold War style mentality about matters related to public diplomacy. It doesn't expand the footprint of public diplomacy to make it everyone's business but rather places emphasis on the commanders and foot soldiers involved in mindspace conflict.

Glassman credits WINEP Executive Director Robert Satloff for many of his own views. Satloff is the author of several books, including *Among the Righteous: Lost Stories from the Holocaust's Long Reach into Arab Lands* and *The Battle of Ideas in the War on Terror: Essays on U.S. Public Diplomacy in the Middle East*. He is the only non-Arab host on an Arab satellite television program, *Dakhil Washington* (Inside Washington), which is syndicated on Al Hurra, the Arab satellite television channel sponsored by the U.S. Government.

In his 2004 book, *The Battle of Ideas in the War on Terror*, Robert Satloff said that much of public diplomacy was wasted spending on Islamists, like trying to get water out of a stone. These were the people to whom President Bush was referring when he asked a question on behalf of the American people:

> *"Americans are asking, why do they hate us? They hate what we see right here in this chamber—a democratically elected government. Their leaders are self-appointed. They hate our freedoms—our freedom of religion, our freedom of speech, our freedom to vote and assemble and disagree with each other. They want to overthrow existing governments in many Muslim countries, such as Egypt, Saudi Arabia, and Jordan. They want to drive Israel out of the Middle East. They want to drive Christians and Jews out of vast regions of*

> *Asia and Africa. These terrorists kill not merely to end lives, but to disrupt and end a way of life."*[37]

Satloff writes: "A relatively small but still sizable, intensely ambitious, and disproportionately powerful subgroup of Muslims do indeed hate 'who we are.' For the most part, these are Islamists—Muslims who reject modern notions of state, citizen, and individual rights and instead seek to impose a totalitarian version of Islam on peoples and nations around the globe. Within this subgroup are those who seek power through revolutionary or violent means and others who seek it through evolutionary or nonviolent means. While the former are unabashed terrorists, it is equally true that the latter can never be democrats."

The Muslim world includes not just the Islamists but also non-Islamist Muslims who are angry and upset about U.S. foreign policies as well as a large segment of Muslims who aren't particularly invested in any cause but are consumed by daily survival. And yet the U.S. public diplomacy approach after 9/11 was to focus on Islamists and keep asking, why do they continue to hate us?

Satloff sees no hope in targeting terrorists with the Muzak version of the information war. Regarding the various stripes of Islamists, the United States can do nothing to soften their hearts or change their minds. "The goal of U.S. policy," he says, "should instead be to seek their defeat—through military means for those who use violence to gain power, and through political means for those whose tactics take a more circuitous path to the same objective. There is no benefit to be gained from targeting public diplomacy toward the Islamists."

"And regarding the millions of poor and struggling Muslims, the goal of U.S. policy should be to help provide them with the economic, educational, social, and other tools required to leave

---

[37] President George W. Bush, Address to Congress, September 20, 2001.

poverty behind and become constructive and contributing members of their societies."

"Without reservation or apology, America's strategy should be to help non- and anti-Islamist Muslims beat back the Islamist challenge. This strategy must be pursued even if many of these putative Muslim allies express bitter dislike for certain aspects of U.S. foreign policy."[38]

Glassman's speech at the Washington Institute made clear his priority as under secretary for public diplomacy and public affairs. "I believe the war of ideas needs urgent attention." His tenure would reflect public service as "the supreme allied commander in the war of ideas," to use the title Senator Joseph Lieberman bestowed upon him at his confirmation hearing in January 2008. Glassman's tenure has been one of urgent crisis communications ever since:

"I am convinced that, unless we get the war of ideas right, we will never succeed in meeting the most significant threat of our time. Unless we get the war of ideas right, the safety of Americans and the future of America's way of life will be in continuous peril."

The context for the war of ideas is public diplomacy. Glassman likes to explain public diplomacy reflexively. "Public diplomacy is diplomacy aimed at publics, as opposed to officials." Public diplomacy is like official diplomacy in mission: the achievement of the national interest. Glassman: "Public diplomacy performs this mission by understanding, informing, engaging, and influencing foreign publics. Ultimately, it is the last word, 'influencing,' that counts most. Our aim is to influence foreign publics to make it easier to achieve U.S. foreign policy goals—both short- and long-term. The key goals today are to diminish the threat to Americans and the rest of the world posed by violent extremism and weapons

---

[38] Robert Satloff, *The Battle of Ideas in the War on Terror: Essays on U.S. Public Diplomacy in the Middle East*, The Washington Institute, 2004.

of mass destruction and to help people around the world achieve freedom."

At one time there was an agency responsible for efforts to inform, engage, and influence foreign publics.

The United States Information Agency was founded in 1953 as an independent agency of the U.S. Government responsible for "telling America's story to the world." Before it was dismantled in October 1999, just two years before the attacks of September 2001, USIA had managed to find a foothold in the post-Cold War era with a shift in focus from ideological gamesmanship to prosperity pitches in the form of pro-NAFTA, pro-Clinton Doctrine story lines. The arsenal of persuasion had become more Commerce Department than Congress of Cultural Freedom and Radio Free Europe. As presidential historian Douglas Brinkley described the Clinton Doctrine in *Foreign Policy* magazine: "Pres. Bill Clinton's foreign policy can be summed up in the words democratic enlargement. It is apparent that economic interests take precedence in Clinton's agenda and that democratic enlargement really means the expansion of global free markets."[39]

I was at USIA during the first two years of the Clinton Administration. Those were heady times. The day after Clinton's election, I went to work as usual at 301 C Street, S.W., only to discover that there were office parties throughout the Agency. Every civil servant seemed to be celebrating the demise of the one-term Bush after the two-term Reagan. We weren't supposed to be partisan while on the job but no one seemed to care that day.

We like to credit Barack Obama as the president of change, but the former Governor of Arkansas along with his youthful vice president Senator Al Gore of Tennessee were the Democratic Rock Stars of their day. They were the dynamic duo men of change. Both

---

[39] Douglas Brinkley, "Democratic Enlargement: The Clinton Doctrine," *Foreign Policy*, March 22, 1997.

Clinton (August 19, 1946) and Gore (March 31, 1948) were the first team candidates for President and Vice President born after World War II. They were respectively 46 and 44 at the time of Inauguration Day 1993. A lot of young voters, including myself, could much more readily identify with these two than their predecessors.

President Clinton represented a generational change from the Reagan-Bush era that looked back more than it looked forward. Clinton was a Georgetown University alumnus in political science with a law degree from Yale. He had learned his political craft from interning in the Senate Foreign Relations office of chairman J. William Fulbright. Senator Fulbright mentored young Clinton and backed his application for a Rhodes Scholarship, the gold standard of sponsored educational exchanges. Clinton, like Obama, served as a law professor, was deemed a master orator like Obama, and very early on in life felt a strong drive as well as a sense of destiny to become his country's leader.

Those of us working at USIA had high hopes for the Clinton approach to public diplomacy. Surely we would make some headway with the youthful president known for his powers of persuasion. Two months after I started working at USIA, I successfully defended my doctoral dissertation on "Fulbright Scholars as Cultural Mediators." In May 1993, I walked across the stage at American University and received my Ph.D. handshake honors from American University President Joseph D. Duffey, who, in just a few weeks, would become the new director of the USIA. Within a short period many of us working on the soft sell side of U.S. foreign policy were hearing rumblings from Capitol Hill that our agency was superfluous in the age of CNN and the World Wide Web. Foreign Relations Chairman Senator Jesse Helms of North Carolina and others seemed to wonder why the American taxpayers were continuing to underwrite America's story when the private market could do it and with more cost savings efficiency? In hindsight it seems incredible that a "One Billion Dollar" agency like

USIA would come up for abolition when U.S. advertising expenditures through mass media campaigns are estimated at $200 billion per year.[40] This 200:1 ratio helped very little to save USIA. How many of us bother writing to the Big Three Automakers asking *them* to stop spending so much commercial TV ad space promoting cars that don't sell?

Duffey was later criticized for not trying to save USIA, especially since he was a longtime FOB (Friend of Bill) going back to his run as Democratic Senator from Connecticut with volunteer help from a young Yale law student, Bill Clinton. Dr. Duffey probably had little control over the demise of USIA. I certainly saw no future at the Agency and by late 1994 I was gone and heading for a career in the academic sector. Seven years later, America's story needed a major overhauling and we awoke to a new emphasis on diplomacy to publics.

The problem in the last seven years is that public diplomacy has become so intertwined with military affairs and war making that it is hard to distinguish the two. Wasn't the military campaign of "Shock and Awe" just a violent version of diplomacy to publics? Here is how CNN reported the first few hours of the invasion of Iraq: "The campaign was intended to instill 'shock and awe' among Iraq's leaders, and it was directed at hundreds of targets in Iraq, officials said. Plumes of fire could be seen rising above targets in Baghdad at 1:05 p.m. EST. CNN Correspondent Wolf Blitzer reported that in his 30 years of experience, he had never seen anything on the scale of Friday's attack on the Iraqi capital."[41]

Brian Whitaker, correspondent for *The Guardian*, reported in 2003: "To some in the Arab and Muslim countries, Shock and Awe

---

[40] Stuart Oskamp and P. Wesley Schultz, *Attitudes and Opinions*, Third Edition, Mahwah, NJ: Lawrence Erlbaum Associates, 2004, 181. "The amount of money devoted to communication and advertising in the United States, and worldwide, is staggering. In the United States, advertising campaigns through the mass media cost over $200 *billion* per year (U.S. Census Bureau, 2002)."

[41] CNN.com, "'Shock and awe' campaign underway in Iraq," March 22, 2003.

is terrorism by another name; to others, a crime that compares unfavourably with September 11."[42]

True to America's genius for marketing anything, in December 2008 an online game called "Sock and Awe" was released as a satire on the shoes-throwing incident during Bush's surprise visit to Baghdad.[43]

Shock and Awe is based on a military doctrine known as Rapid Dominance. Here is how its authors Ullman and Wade describe its purpose:

> *"The aim of Rapid Dominance is to affect the will, perception, and understanding of the adversary to fit or respond to our strategic policy ends through imposing a regime of Shock and Awe. Clearly, the traditional military aim of destroying, defeating, or neutralizing the adversary's military capability is a fundamental and necessary component of Rapid Dominance. Our intent, however, is to field a range of capabilities to induce sufficient Shock and Awe to render the adversary impotent. This means that physical and psychological effects must be obtained."*[44]

Ullman cites the German *blitzkrieg* and the dropping of nuclear bombs on the Japanese cities of Hiroshima and Nagasaki as precursors to this level of total devastation to enemy populations. Any cursory observer of history knows that such total warfare also wreaked utter death and destruction on civilian populations.

> *"The key objective of Rapid Dominance is to impose this overwhelming level of Shock and Awe against an adversary on an immediate or sufficiently timely basis to paralyze its will to carry on. In crude terms, Rapid Dominance would seize control of the environment and paralyze or so overload an*

---

[42] Brian Whitaker, "Flags in the dust," *The Guardian*, March 24, 2003.
[43] www.sockandawe.com
[44] Harlan Ullman, James P. Wade, *et al, Shock and Awe: Achieving Rapid Dominance*, National Defense University, Institute for National Strategic Studies, The Center for Advanced Concepts and Technology, 1996, xxiv.

adversary's perceptions and understanding of events so that the enemy would be incapable of resistance at tactical and strategic levels. An adversary would be rendered totally impotent and vulnerable to our actions."[45]

Harlan Ullman has distanced himself from the Shock and Awe campaign used during Operation Iraqi Freedom. He is an affiliated adviser and expert with the Center for Strategic and International Studies (CSIS) and retired Commander in the U.S. Navy. He wrote this in a 2005 collection of essays entitled *Owls and Eagles*:

> *Often amused and occasionally angered by Washington's pet classification of people as "hawks" or "doves," a mindless categorization when you think about it especially since many of this administration's toughest hawks avoided rigorous military experience and its chief doves not only fought in war but were wounded in action, "owls" and eagles" seemed a more sensible alternative as well as a slightly unsubtle form of derision. Owls are far tougher and brighter than doves. Eagles are immensely more formidable and powerful than hawks. The meaning was clear: U.S. policy should be smart, informed by fact and reason and not ideology, and tough when it must be. Those ends have not been met particularly when it comes to keeping the nation safe and secure. Consider Iraq.*
>
> *Intelligence misjudgments are often common. It is a tough business. However, in this case, ideology as presented by the so-called 'neo-conservatives' and which asserted that democratization of the Greater Middle East provided practical one- stop strategic shopping to correct the ills of that troubled and violent region, prevailed in capturing the president. That fact can prove to be the biggest strategic blunder of this or any other century in the nation's history."*[46]

---

[45] Ullman, *Shock and Awe*, xv-xvi.

[46] Harlan K. Ullman, *Owls and Eagles: Ending the Foreign Policy Flights of Fancy of Hawks, Doves, and Neo-cons*, Lanham, MD: Rowman & Littlefield, 2005, xi-xii.

His latest book is *America's Promise Restored: Preventing Culture, Crusade, and Partisanship from Wrecking Our Nation* (Carroll & Graf, 2006) that is described as "a provocative analysis of why our government is broken and what needs to be done to make it work again." In an email exchange December 24, 2008, I asked Ullman about whether or not he supports James Glassman's war of ideas philosophy. He does. "You need to take a look at what the Department of Defense Science Board wrote about this in September 2004. It was titled Strategic Communication and its thesis was that we cannot win the war on terror unless we win the war on ideas and we are losing that battle---a remarkably candid and refreshing study that in my view was on the mark then and more so today---even though we have done nothing of weight or moment."

I recall this 111-page report very well. It offers a foreshadowing of Glassman's approach to public diplomacy four years later:

> *Strategic communication is a vital component of U.S. national security. It is in crisis, and it must be transformed with a strength of purpose that matches our commitment to diplomacy, defense, intelligence, law enforcement, and homeland security. Presidential leadership and the bipartisan political will of Congress are essential. Collaboration between government and the private sector on an unprecedented scale is imperative.*
>
> *To succeed, we must understand the United States is engaged in a generational and global struggle about ideas, not a war between the West and Islam. It is more than a war against the tactic of terrorism. We must think in terms of global networks, both government and non-government. If we continue to concentrate primarily on states ("getting it*

> *right" in Iraq, managing the next state conflict better), we will fail.*[47]

Among other things, the Defense Science Board recommended that public diplomacy, PSYOPS (psychological operations), open military operations and public affairs "must be coordinated and energized." Further, the report states that the war of ideas begins at the top and does not bubble up from the grassroots. "A unifying vision of strategic communication starts with Presidential direction. Only White House leadership, with support from cabinet secretaries and Congress, can bring about the sweeping reforms that are required." This makes sense today for a globally sophisticated ideas-driven president like Barack Obama. It did not make sense in 2004 for a presidential leader like George W. Bush who had an understanding of war, albeit poorly understood in hindsight, but who drew a blank about how to rescue American credibility from the abyss.

The Strategic Communication report emphasizes prioritizing communications and public opinion analysis in all aspects of policy making. Published just a month after Barack Obama impressed fellow Democrats with his moving speech at the Democratic Convention in August 2004, this excerpt seems to be directed at our 44th president:

> *Nothing shapes U.S. policies and global perceptions of U.S. foreign and national security objectives more powerfully than the President's statements and actions, and those of senior officials. Interests, not public opinion, should drive policies. But opinions must be taken into account when policy options are considered and implemented. At a minimum, we should not be surprised by public reactions to policy choices.*

---

[47] Report of the Defense Science Board Task Force on Strategic Communication, Office of the Under Secretary of Defense For Acquisition, Technology, and Logistics
Washington, D.C. 20301-3140, September 2004, 2.

> *Policies will not succeed unless they are communicated to global and domestic audiences in ways that are credible and allow them to make informed, independent judgments. Words in tone and substance should avoid offence where possible; messages should seek to reduce, not increase, perceptions of arrogance, opportunism, and double standards. These objectives mean officials must take full advantage of powerful tools to measure attitudes, understand cultures, and assess influence structures—not occasionally but as an iterative process. Policies and \strategic communication cannot be separated.*[48]

Clausewitz said, "War is diplomacy by other means." The *Art of War* Chinese writer Sun Tzu inspired the "selective, instant decapitation of military or societal targets to achieve shock and awe." Ullman cites Sun Tzu's efforts to turn the king's concubines into good soldiers. Create a precise marching troop, said the king to Suz Tzu. The concubines did not follow Sun Tzu's orders so he decapitated the lead concubine in front of the others. The women still hesitated so he lobbed off a second head. They soon marched in precision. Shock and awe, then and now. If those dicta still hold today, then public diplomacy in the age of Bush was utilized as just another means to gain military and national security advantage in the War on Terror and wars in Afghanistan and Iraq. In the age of Obama, there may be an opportunity to use total information spectrum public diplomacy without doing damage to our reputation for double talk and overkill that the U.S. earned over the last 8 years.

Today the United States continues to approach public diplomacy through a military lens. While there is now more bipartisan commitment to public diplomacy expansion, the biggest cheerleading for public diplomacy comes from inside the corridors of the Pentagon. As Glassman notes, "One of the biggest

---

[48] Strategic Communication, 3.

enthusiasts for public diplomacy in government is the secretary of defense." He's referring to Secretary of Defense Robert Gates, who was CIA Director under the first President Bush. The former SECDEF was Donald Rumsfeld who regularly promoted the expansion of the information war spectrum and strategic communication.[49]

Persuader-in-Chief Barack Obama is in the best position of any president since Dwight Eisenhower or Ronald Reagan of making a serious commitment to public diplomacy and strategic communication in the post-Bush II years. He has enormous advantages that include a disciplined, on-message approach to explaining his policies to both the American people and the rest of the world. He has the benefit of the honeymoon period that will follow from his historic election and personal charm and likeability. He's most obviously an intellectually curious president and a fresh change from the absolutist, uncurious ideologue who preceded him. He's been called the "great reconciler" for his keen ability to play to strengths across the political spectrum.

Obama stated several times as a presidential candidate that he will not rule by ideology, but pragmatism. In speaking about his Brain Trust, he said, "We're not an ideological people. We're a commonsense people who say, 'What's going to work?' and 'Let's figure it out.'"[50] This sounds convincing until one looks at his voting record in the Senate. The nonpartisan *National Journal* deemed Obama the most liberal Senator in 2007.[51] Hillary Clinton was ranked the 16th most liberal Senator in 2007. This candidate ran on

---

[49] Strategic Communication is the "synchronized coordination of statecraft, public affairs, public diplomacy, military information operations, and other activities, reinforced by political, economic, military and other actions, to advance foreign policy interests." Put simply, it is the ability to coordinate and synchronize a clear, articulate message of your organization's goals, policies and values to global publics.

[50] "What Obama Means for Business," Nina Easton, *Fortune*, July 7, 2008, 72.

[51] "Obama: Most Liberal Senator In 2007," Brian Friel, Richard E. Cohen and Kirk Victor, *National Journal*, Jan. 31, 2008.

a promise that he would raise taxes on the wealthiest Americans and raise the federal minimum wage to nearly $10 over the next two years. Candidate Obama explained his positions to reporters and the fence sitters that prosperity in America rises from the bottom up so it's the bottom of America that needs the most attention. Given the inability of his opponent John McCain to mount any sound alternative to Obama on the growing economic debacle in 2008, Obama won the presidency on this progressive pitch too.

As a candidate, Obama did reassure Wall Street and American capitalists that "I still believe that the business of America is business. But what I also think is that with all that power and talent, and all those resources at their disposal, comes some responsibilities—to not game the system, to not oppose increased transparency in the marketplace, to not oppose fiscally prudent measures to balance the budget."[52] His choice of Clinton administration alumni Robert Rubin and Lawrence Summers as inner circle financial advisers caused concern to his liberal/left base that worked so hard to elect him. Summers was a particularly controversial choice. As Harvard University president, Summers was accused of making sexist remarks about women's intellectual abilities in the hard sciences. (His comment was a statistical one: men's intelligence varies more than women's. In this view, there are more extremely intellectual men, and there are also more extremely dumb men. I don't know if this is a win for women.) More disturbing, as a World Bank chief economist, Summers had suggested in a memorandum to a colleague that the U.S. consider shipping toxic waste to countries in Africa. "I've always though that under-populated countries in Africa are vastly under-polluted, their air quality is probably vastly inefficiently low compared to Los Angeles or Mexico City." That was in 1991 and one should always give people second chances. In this case, I would recommend that

---

[52] Easton, 72.

Summers remain a behind-the-scenes adviser just in case he has a sudden outburst of inanity like he did while at the World Bank.

The American electorate chose Obama over McCain, and it wasn't due at all to his liberal voting record in Congress. It seems to have been despite his left-liberal heart that Obama was elected. The American people were tired of being talked down to or dismissed by the Bush-Cheney administration and chose a candidate who talked about how he would do everything in his power to restore America's greatness, even if it might mean an economic recovery program that FDR would envy. Further, Obama did much to allay fears that he might be too liberal for the presidency by expanding his Cabinet and inner circle of advisers far outside the Democratic Party.

So what might President Obama do for the war of ideas? Based on his prioritizing of the economy in the first 100 days, it is likely that Obama's approach to public diplomacy and strategic communication may be along the lines of the Hippocratic oath: First, do no harm. As one who has spent the last decade and a half working in this area, I hope that the president will enlist an expanded network of government, private sector, private citizen, and academic advisers who can take a long, hard look at all the tools of public diplomacy. Make public diplomacy everyone's business so that one day we can say, the business of America includes public diplomacy and not just business.

One signal of Obama's approach to public diplomacy is his decision to keep Secretary of Defense Robert M. Gates in place for his new term. Gates gave a powerful case for the importance of soft power *and* smart power in the Landon Lecture at Kansas State University in November 2007:

> *My message is that if we are to meet the myriad challenges around the world in the coming decades, this country must strengthen other important elements of national power both institutionally and financially, and*

> *create the capability to integrate and apply all of the elements of national power to problems and challenges abroad. In short, based on my experience serving seven presidents, as a former Director of CIA and now as Secretary of Defense, I am here to make the case for strengthening our capacity to use "soft" power and for better integrating it with "hard" power.*
>
> *One of the most important lessons of the wars in Iraq and Afghanistan is that military success is not sufficient to win: economic development, institution- building and the rule of law, promoting internal reconciliation, good governance, providing basic services to the people, training and equipping indigenous military and police forces, strategic communications, and more—these, along with security, are essential ingredients for long-term success.*[53]

Gates is a self-described "old Cold Warrior with a doctorate in history." He bemoans the abolition of key agencies like USIA that helped shepherd national government powers of persuasion:

> *The Marshall Plan and later the United States Agency for International \Development acknowledged the role of economics in the world; the CIA the role of intelligence; and the United States Information Agency the fact that the conflict would play out as much in hearts and minds as it would on any battlefield.*
>
> *The key, over time, was to devote the necessary resources -people and money - and get enough things right while maintaining the ability to recover from mistakes along the way. Ultimately, our endurance paid off and the Soviet Union crumbled, and the decades-long Cold War ended.*
>
> *However, during the 1990s, with the complicity of both the Congress and the White House, key instruments of*

---

[53] Secretary of State Robert M. Gates, Landon Lecture, Kansa State University, Manhattan, Kansa, November 26, 2007; http://www.defenselink.mil/speeches/speech.aspx?speechid=1199

America's national power once again were allowed to wither or were abandoned. Most people are familiar with cutbacks in the military and intelligence – including sweeping reductions in manpower, nearly 40 percent in the active army, 30 percent in CIA's clandestine service and spies.

What is not as well-known, and arguably even more shortsighted, was the gutting of America's ability to engage, assist, and communicate with other parts of the world— the "soft power," which had been so important throughout the Cold War. The State Department froze the hiring of new Foreign Service officers for a period of time. The United States Agency for International Development saw deep staff cuts— its permanent staff dropping from a high of 15,000 during Vietnam to about 3,000 in the 1990s. And the U.S. Information Agency was abolished as an independent entity, split into pieces, and many of its capabilities folded into a small corner of the State Department.

With Gates in place, and if James Glassman stays on as undersecretary of state for public diplomacy, we know what will prevail in the age of Obama: international broadcasting, new media, and exchanges. Glassman sits on the Broadcasting Board of Governors as the Secretary of State's representative. He is quite sanguine about taxpayer-funded international broadcasting:

The state of our broadcasting effort is healthy. Every week, 175 million adults around the world tune in to programming—in a total of 60 languages—from Voice of America, Radio Free Europe/Radio Liberty, Al Hurra, Radio Sawa, Radio and TV Marti and Radio Free Asia. That is a 75 percent increase in audience since 2002. Of the 75 million new listeners and viewers, about half are Arabic speakers. The BBG is having an impact in places like Tibet, Burma, Kenya, North Korea, Cuba, and Iran. In Iran, VOA Persian TV broadcasts seven hours a day and reaches more than one-quarter of adult Iranians by satellite. Al Hurra has a bigger audience than al-Jazeera in Iraq and is viewed each week by more than half the adults in Syria. One reason the *broadcasting effort works is that it has a clear and \ limited mission. It is effective, but it is only one tool.*[54]

I am less sanguine about all aspects of international broadcasting. I believe the Voice of America is a good public asset of the United States and warrants expansion. I've had many conversations with VOA staff and alumni who are dismayed at the crippling of this World War II asset. VOA is no BBC, nor could it ever be, but it operates like the BBC as a quasi-governmental broadcast organization. Credibility is everything to VOA and its charter is very clear about this:

The long-range interests of the United States are served by communicating directly with the peoples of the world by radio. To be effective, the Voice of America must win the attention and respect of listeners. These principles will therefore govern Voice of America (VOA) broadcasts. 1. VOA will serve as a consistently reliable and authoritative source of news. VOA news will be accurate, objective, and comprehensive. 2. VOA will represent America, not any single segment of American society, and will therefore present a balanced and comprehensive projection of significant American thought and institutions. 3. VOA will present the policies of the United States clearly and effectively, and will also present responsible discussions and opinion on these policies.

I have worked with the Voice of America in radio and television over many years and have always found the employees to be courteous and professional. There is nothing overtly propagandistic about VOA, but still today few Americans know anything about VOA or its broadcast operations due to Congressional mandate, notably the Smith-Mundt Act of 1948 that prohibits US Government rebroadcast of programming designed strictly for an overseas audience. I invite my readers to take a look at the Voice of

[54] James Glassman, "Winning the War of Ideas," speech at the Washington Institute for Near East Policy, July 2008.

America We site by visiting www.voanews.com, which is not governed by the anachronistic legislation.

Al Hurra, Radio Sawa, Radio/TV Marti, and other Cold War/War on Terror symbols need a public hearing in Congress.

I beam with lioness pride at Glassman's remarks about educational and cultural programs of the State Department: "Within the State Department itself, the crown jewels of public diplomacy are our educational and cultural exchange programs, where we spend the majority of State's diplomacy funds. To the rest of the world, higher education is America's greatest brand, and, despite tighter visa requirements since 9/11, the school year 2007-08 produced a record number of international students coming to the U.S. to study, about 600,000 of them—a dramatic recovery. The U.S. is far and away the most desirable destination in the world for learning."[55]

In the age of Obama, international educational and cultural exchange should have resources that match their crown jewel status. The Fulbright Program, of which I am an alumna, and the International Visitor Leadership Program deserve at least a doubling in funding. The IVLP sponsors about 5,000 visitors per year and boasts a litany of well-heeled graduates, including over 290 Chiefs of State and Heads of Government, as well as 2,000 Cabinet-level officials. IVLP alumni include Tony Blair, Oscar Sanchez, Hamid Karzai, Nikolas Sarkozy, and Margaret Thatcher.

In an economically stable U.S., I'd call for a tenfold increase. I was not only a Fulbright scholar to the Federal Republic of Germany but also the Fulbright desk officer for Germany, Spain, and the former Yugoslavia countries. I also had the great privilege of meeting Senator J. William Fulbright on several occasions, including an interview I conducted with Senator Fulbright for *Washington International* magazine in his downtown Washington,

---

[55] Glassman, July 2008.

DC law office shortly after Bill Clinton's election in 1992. Fulbright was a great ambassador for educational exchange and when he died at the age of 89 in February 1995, America lost its last great international education advocate. No one has emerged since, though before his death, Senator Paul Simon (D-Illinois) was an outspoken proponent of expanding international exchange opportunities for young Americans. That other former Senator from Illinois should revisit the recommendations his dear friend and early supporter Paul Simon had for creating something akin to a Marshall Plan of International Exchange and Ideas. A great start would be the passage of the Senator Paul Simon Study Abroad Foundation Act whose program goals include the following:

> *Establish an innovative public-private partnership to create a more globally informed American citizenry by:*
>
> - *Increasing participation in quality study abroad programs.*
> - *Encouraging diversity in student participation in study abroad.*
> - *Diversifying locations of study abroad, particularly in developing countries.*
> - *Making study abroad a cornerstone of today's higher education.*[56]

In addition to educational and cultural exchange, traditional public diplomacy efforts supported by the State Department are English teaching programs, many of which are emphasizing teaching English to disadvantaged youth in Muslim countries. State also sends out about 800 American experts per year in various key fields deemed important to policy goals in target countries. This is the information side about America, letting others learn from us and about us directly from our citizens, the people-to-people

---

[56] See NAFSA Web site, http://www.nafsa.org/public_policy.sec/commission_on_the_abraham/

exchange of information that is a mainstay of good public diplomacy efforts.

The current undersecretary of State for public diplomacy Glassman sees his role as both a day-to-day manager of State Department-sponsored public diplomacy efforts, but also as the war of ideas persuader-in-chief. In April 2006, President Bush asked then under secretary of state for public diplomacy Karen Hughes to coordinate the interagency efforts in the war of ideas. She and her successor Glassman head a Policy Coordinating Committee (PCC) that includes representatives from across government, including State, Defense, CIA, Homeland Security, Treasury, Justice, USAID, and the BBG.

The war of ideas is focused squarely on counterterrorism and winning the war on terror. To quote Glassman, "As the National Strategy for Combating Terrorism of 2006 puts it: 'In the long run, winning the War on Terror means winning the battle of ideas.'"

The war of ideas under George W. Bush is a marked contrast in spirit and style to the Jimmy Carter era of the U.S. Information Agency. Carter, the president who emphasized a human rights approach to foreign policy, endorsed having the name of the Agency changed from the US Information Agency to the International Communications Agency (ICA) in 1978, which came about with the merger of USIA and the State Department's Bureau of Educational and Cultural Affairs.

Figure 4. Jimmy Carter

Here is how the USIA explained this name change:

> *Another major USIA reorganization, approved in 1977 by President Jimmy Carter, took effect on April 1, 1978. The State Department's Bureau of Educational and Cultural Affairs and USIA were combined as the United States International Communication Agency (USICA). President Carter's definition of the agency's mission, transmitted to Congress in 1977, added a second mandate for the agency. It stated that the Agency's principal function should be "to reduce the degree to which misperceptions and misunderstandings complicate relations between the United States and other nations. It is also in our interest--and in the interest of other nations--that Americans have the opportunity to understand the histories, cultures, and problems of others, so that we can come to understand their hopes, perceptions, and aspirations."*[57]

Historian Nicholas Cull writes that Carter "had a particular interest in one area of public diplomacy: international exchanges. In 1972, as governor of Georgia, he traveled to Latin America with the State Department's 'Partners of the Americas' program. The experience had been a personal summons to action. In office, Carter strengthened international exchange provisions. He ensured that ICA's mission statement stressed 'mutuality,' as he intended that the United States as well as the foreign partner would be enriched by these exchanges. This emphasis on reaching the home audience became known within the agency as the 'second,' 'reverse,' or 'two-way mandate.'"[58] ICA reflected the two-way mandate of the Agency, which was not only to tell America's story to the world, but also to introduce the world to America and thereby promote mutual understanding.

---

[57] See "USIA's Reorganization" at http://dosfan.lib.uic.edu/usia/usiahome/oldoview.htm#overview.

[58] Nicholas J. Cull, *The Cold War and the United States Information Agency: American Propaganda and Public Diplomacy, 1945-1989* (New York: Cambridge University Press, 2008), 361.

Consider USIA's longtime mission: "To understand, inform, and influence foreign publics in promotion of the national interest, and to broaden the dialogue between Americans and U.S. institutions, and their counterparts abroad." Its stated goals were: (1) To explain and advocate U.S. policies in terms that are credible and meaningful in foreign cultures; (2) To provide information about the official policies of the United States, and about the people, values, and institutions which influence those policies; (3) To bring the benefits of international engagement to American citizens and institutions by helping them build strong long-term relationships with their counterparts overseas; and (4) To advise the President and U.S. government policy-makers on the ways in which foreign attitudes will have a direct bearing on the effectiveness of U.S. policies.[59]

Jimmy Carter sought to put more weight into goal three. His own exchange experience taught him the value of relationship building with counterparts overseas. It's a value that Carter has extended all the way up to today, with his continued monitoring of international elections and Carter Center work on combating life-threatening diseases in the developing world.

Carter's one-term presidency was defined by information outreach and the personal touch. Even his inauguration parade was historic. I recall watching as Carter and his family got out of their armored limousine to walk the last stretch of the parade along Pennsylvania Avenue. It was astonishing at the time and seemed careless or even hokey. I did not realize then that this gesture alone symbolized a president who saw himself as a man of the people. He did not want America portrayed to the world as an arrogant power. Rather, he pledged to overcome cynicism and malaise, and Watergate's stain. Carter's inaugural address pledged that America would run its policy through best principles:

---

[59] See "USIA: An Overview" at http://dosfan.lib.uic.edu/usia/usiahome/oldoview.htm#overview.

Ours was the first society openly to define itself in terms of both spirituality and of human liberty. It is that unique self-definition which has given us an exceptional appeal, but it also imposes on us a special obligation, to take on those moral duties which, when assumed, seem invariably to be in our own best interests.

Our Nation can be strong abroad only if it is strong at home. And we know that the best way to enhance freedom in other lands is to demonstrate here that our democratic system is worthy of emulation.

To be true to ourselves, we must be true to others. We will not behave in foreign places so as to violate our rules and standards here at home, for we know that the trust which our Nation earns is essential to our strength.

USIA prepared a multilingual four-part video series called *Transition 77* and distributed a five-minute inaugural message for the world in which Carter called on the world community to unite "in a common effort based on mutual trust and mutual respect."[60] Mutuality was the key ingredient of Carter's approach to public diplomacy.

Figure 5. Ronald Reagan

[60] As quoted in Nicholas J. Cull, *The Cold War and the United States Information Agency: American Propaganda and Public Diplomacy, 1945-1989* (New York: Cambridge University Press, 2008), 360.

Within two years after Ronald Reagan was elected in November 1980, the agency's name was restored to USIA. ICA sounded too much like CIA, and the Cold War struggle between the US and USSR was taking precedence over a global community based on mutual trust. The American electorate did not reelect the idealistic Democrat Carter whose handling of the Americans held hostage in Iran turned out to be a fiasco, nor did they want someone who acknowledged a perpetuating malaise in the culture. Carter seemed almost too soft for the job of president. The public preferred the ideological warrior Reagan who promised morning in America and a restoration of American superiority around the world. Reagan himself wrote in a letter, "We are determined to *stop* losing the propaganda war."[61] Charles Z. Wick, a longtime FOR (Friend of Ron), came from Hollywood to Washington determined to give USIA a new seat at the ideological table. He didn't have to push that hard. Reagan promised change as a candidate:

> *It's time to expand dramatically the Voice of America, Radio Free Europe and Radio Liberty. We have a message of peace and hope and nothing to be ashamed of in the examples we set for the world. Millions upon millions of people look to us as a beacon of freedom in a world that is fast losing freedom. We can convey our own deep convictions to the world to combat the hostile and ceaseless communist propaganda that distorts everything we stand for.*[62]

Some scholars credit Reagan with his fundamentalist approach to American superiority. Joseph Loconte of Pepperdine University writes:

> *Though alternately chided as a "warmonger," a "washed-up actor," or a "happy dunce," Reagan advanced a foreign policy doctrine of confronting Soviet aggression that proved*

[61] Ronald Reagan, *Reagan: A Life in Letters* (Detroit: Free Press, 2003), 376.
[62] Ronald Reagan, Lincoln Day dinner remarks, Worchester, Massachusetts, February 1980. See also Lou Cannon, "Reagan's Foreign Policy: Scrap 'Weakness, Illusion,' Stress Military Strength," *Washington Post*, February 16, 1980, A3.

> *immensely prescient and effective. His approach to negotiations with Soviet leader Mikhail Gorbachev—"trust but verify"—reduced the risk of nuclear war by reducing the means of waging war. Reagan rejected the conventional wisdom that a nation's behavior, and not its political ideology, mattered most. "Our military strength is a prerequisite to peace, but let it be clear we maintain this strength in the hope it will never be used," he said, "for the ultimate determinant in the struggle that's now going on in the world will not be bombs and rockets but a test of wills and ideas, a trial of spiritual resolve, the values we hold, the beliefs we cherish, the ideals to which we are dedicated." Three years after Ronald Reagan left office, the collapse of the Soviet empire was complete.*[63]

I was a moderate supporter of Reagan his first term and a critic of him his second term. By then I was living abroad in Europe as a Fulbright scholar to the Federal Republic of Germany and shared the sentiment of many Europeans that Reagan was a bit off his rocker. On August 11, 1984, days into my sojourn in Germany, Reagan made his "joke" during a mic check. "My fellow Americans, I'm pleased to tell you that I've just signed legislation that will outlaw Russia forever. We begin bombing in five minutes."[64] There was legitimate fear that Reagan was out of touch with negative global opinion and had been reduced to cupping his hand to his ear in response to shouting reporters or releasing deflecting zingers. His aggressive posture toward the Communist regime in Moscow was quite popular in the Eastern satellite countries.

Charles Z. Wick had his own problems in 1984. A story was leaked to the press that the Reagan administration's USIA had been keeping a list of nearly 100 Americans deemed unsuitable for

---

[63] Joseph Loconte, "American Presidents and the American Creed," America in the World Journal, August 14, 2008; http://americaintheworld.typepad.com.

[64] "President's Joke about Bombing Leaves Press in Europe Un-amused," *The New York Times*, Associate Press Wire Story, August 14, 1984, A8.

participation in its speakers bureau, American Participants (Amparts) program. The blacklist included prominent journalists, authors, and activists such as Walter Cronkite, Coretta Scott King, and Ralph Nader, as well foreign policy leaders such as Madeleine Albright and McGeorge Bundy.[65] Though Wick decried the existence of such a list when it was revealed during an internal audit, the public exposure was personally embarrassing and for a time Wick seemed on the verge of resigning. He emerged from this nadir as arguably the most powerful director in USIA's history. Wick and Reagan were a team dedicated to the force of public diplomacy.

---

[65] Howard Kurtz, "USIA Blacklisted Liberals from Speaking Engagements Abroad," *Washington Post*, February 9, 1984, A2.

ORANGE JUICE AND LEMONADE

James Glassman has a citrus vision. He shares a Charles Z. Wick-like focused commitment to the war of ideas, "to use the tools of ideological engagement—words, deeds, and images—to create an environment hostile to violent extremism. We want to break the linkages between groups like al-Qaeda and their target audiences." Just as with the Communist ideology and propaganda directed at the United States for nearly 50 years, both James Glassman and Defense Secretary Robert Gates believe that if the U.S. does not isolate and marginalize violent extremists, including terrorist organizations and individuals, the foundation of our American freedoms will give way.

But is the war of ideas public diplomacy or military information operations? Glassman:

> *"Unlike traditional functions of public diplomacy like education and cultural exchanges, the aim of the war of ideas is not to persuade foreign populations to adopt more favorable views of the United States and its policies. Instead, the war of ideas tries to ensure that negative sentiments and day-to-day grievances toward the United States and its allies do not manifest themselves in the form of violent extremism."*

Brand America or restoring America's image in the world is not a war of ideas priority.

The battle within the Muslim world today is. To put it bluntly, he says,

> *"This is a battle in which we cannot be a bystander if we wanted to. We cannot step aside and simply watch Muslims slug it out among themselves. Instead, the battle within the Muslim world for power affects the United States directly and was responsible for the deaths of 3,000 people seven years ago. In this battle, our main role is to support constructive alternatives to violent extremism...Our priority is not to promote our brand but to help destroy theirs."*

Glassman concludes with a thirst-quenching analogy:

> *Think of America's values and political system as orange juice; think of the al-Qaeda system of violent extremism as lemonade. Our job for the short term is not to put all of our efforts into getting people to drink orange juice, but to get them not to drink lemonade. They can drink anything else they want: milk, ginger ale, tomato juice, Coke. We are confident that, ultimately, they will come around to orange juice or something close to it, but in the meantime, we want them to stay away from lemonade.*

The U.S. may not need to worry so much at least for now about winning a global popularity contest. We've already won with Obama. This is not to say that Obama's win will give U.S. foreign policy a pass in the world. The December 2008 war in Israel between the Hamas-backed fighters in Gaza and the Israeli Defense Forces has placed the U.S. squarely in the middle of the ongoing Middle East conflict, though tilting in the Israeli direction. U.S. support for Israel remains unpopular among Muslims and Arabs, but also among many Europeans who believe that the U.S. government will not act as a balanced mediator in the conflict. President Obama's strong support for Israel makes him less than a Rock Star in these circles, even if many Muslims are proud of Obama's familial Muslim heritage.

So which public diplomacy platform will prevail in an Obama era? Will it be Glassman's approach that emphasizes defanging violent extremists even if America's reputation suffers? Glassman underscores his position with the words of Rob Satloff: "The 'battle of ideas' is not a popularity contest about us; it is a battle for political power among Muslims, in which America's favorability rating is irrelevant." Or will public diplomacy emphasize soft power strategies that are designed to get others to want to be more like us? It's impossible to predict, other than to say that given the global financial crisis, the battle of ideas will be tempered by declining resources, which in turn will trickle down and impact all the other traditional public diplomacy efforts in broadcasting and exchanges.

The most credible voices in the war of ideas, Glassman admits, will not be those of the Americans, but other Muslims. The biggest battles are being fought right now within Muslim and Arab societies or areas with significant Muslim and Arab populations that struggle for identity within multiethnic societies (Mumbai).

Glassman's American war of ideas manifesto ends with this ultimate goal: A world in which the use of violence to achieve political, religious, or social objectives is no longer considered acceptable; efforts to radicalize and recruit new members are no longer successful; and the perpetrators of violent extremism are condemned and isolated.

To achieve this goal, he suggests that the U.S. use the powerful persuasion device known as diversion. Keep potential violent extremist recruits out of trouble through "the attractions of entertainment, culture, literature, music technology, sports, education, business and culture, in addition to politics and religion." He also has announced the contemporary version of the successful *Problems of Communism* USIA journal published during the Cold War. The publisher M.E. Sharpe has published its successor, *Problems of Post-Communism*, since 1992. The 21st century version, Problems of Extremism, will be available in hard copy and online and serve as a guidepost for ongoing dialogue and conferences. It will not be run by the State Department but rather directed by European think tank scholars supported with public and private funds. Glassman, like Obama, wants to tap into all the existing social media Web sites and make goals compatible with Web 2.0 platforms.

James Glassman also advocates the creation of virtual and real countermovements along the lines of a Mothers Against Drunk Driving (MADD) model that would bring like-minded people together in a spirit of resolve and unity against violent extremists in their communities. The U.S. role in that operation is "as a facilitator of choice. Mainly behind the scenes, we help build networks and movements—put tools in the hands of young people to make their own choices, rather than dictating those choices. Again, in the words of the National Security Strategy: 'Freedom cannot be imposed; it must be chosen.'"

> *"I want to stress that we are on the lookout for measures that marry the traditional means of public diplomacy with the war of ideas effort. One idea: a far more robust alumni network—encouraging social networking by Internet among the one million alumni participants in our educational and cultural exchange programs. If they wish to help, these alumni will be credible voices, pushing back against violent extremism and offering alternatives."*

In November 2008, the United States elected a very public-service oriented president, Barack Obama. He emphasizes transparency, ongoing interaction between the governing and the governed, and a renewed trust in government to serve as a helpmate to those in need. Given that background, how many of us will jump on the war of ideas effort? We may be worrying more now about pocketbook issues such as jobs, healthcare, and mortgages, than a pushback against violent extremism. But we have to heed the future and become more like Faith Popcorn in predicting what's around the corner a mere decade or two away. Consider this prediction from the National Intelligence Council report, "Global Trends 2025: A Transformed World."

> *By 2025, nation-states will no longer be the only—and often not the most important—actors on the world stage and the "international system" will have morphed to accommodate the new reality. But the transformation will be incomplete and uneven. Although states will not disappear from the international scene, the relative power of various nonstate actors—including businesses, tribes, religious organizations, and even criminal networks—will grow as*

> *these groups influence decisions on a widening range of social, economic, and political issues.*[66]

Cataclysmic events like the recent attacks in Mumbai and the conflict in the Gaza strip in Israel will shift public opinion immediately from economic and personal security to national security.

[66] National Intelligence Council, "Global Trends 2025: A Transformed World," December 2008; available online at www.dni.gov/nic/NIC_2025_project.html

MINISTRY OF AMERICAN CULTURE (MAC) DADDY

Figure 6. Louis Armstrong

As I've written this book, I've been listening to a lot of American music, everything from Hip Hop and R&B music by local Syracuse, New York independent performing artists Herizon, Anna "Nyanna" Patterson and Innasense to American musical theater like Judy Garland and Jane Froman as well as Black Soul Music. The twenty-volume set, "Soul Hits of the 70s: Didn't It Blow Your Mind," released by Rhino Records in the 1990s is a particularly prized jewel of the era. The talent base in American music history is mind-blowing. Where do we begin or end? From Johnny Cash and Sam Cooke to Stevie Wonder and Aretha Franklin, Marvin Gaye and Tami Terrell, to Curtis Mayfield, Gladys Knight to Otis Redding. The list is endless. Even Cher is an American cultural classic who has used her celebrity status to do good works for war veterans in the post-9/11 era.

Think of what the United States of America, particularly Black Americans, have contributed to the world in art, music and culture. Just follow the Blues Trail that runs from the backside of Memphis, Tennessee along Highway 61 and part of Highway 49 through the Mississippi Delta region of the American South.[67] I recall walking into the Beale Street studio of Ernest C. Withers, an African-American photographer who documented the rise of a number of Sun Record veterans, including Elvis Presley and B.B. King. How I met Ernest begins near the Blues Trail in Oxford, Mississippi.

It was May 2002 and I had just finished a Knight Foundation Fellowship on "The Fourth Estate and the Third Sector" at the University of Mississippi (Ole Miss). One of our local cultural excursions included a stop in Clarksdale, Mississippi, the heart of the Delta Blues Trail. We dined at an upscale restaurant, Madidi, owned by the actor and Greenwood, Mississippi native, Morgan Freeman, and danced at his downscale Ground Zero Blues Club, created to have the look and feel of a days-gone-by joint, complete with homemade-style fried chicken and apple cobbler. We toured the Delta Blues Museum, located in a 1918 former railroad depot, where you can take a look inside the actual cabin where Muddy Waters was born.

We also took in a special exhibit of photographs at Southside Gallery located on Oxford Square. The gallery owner and artist Milly Moorhead[68] was displaying photographs by Memphis native, Ernest C. Withers. The wall was covered with pictures that told America's story, including one of a woman smiling broadly in her Sunday best, holding up her voter registration card to the camera. There was a picture of the King family sitting on the front row at Dr. King's funeral. I assumed this American storyteller was long dead, which is my tendency whenever I see something so

---

[67] See Mississippi Blues Trail Commission; http://www.msbluestrail.org/blues_trail/

[68] Learn more about Milly Moorhead West at www.cubawest.com

remarkable that stops me in my tracks. I remarked how great it would have been to meet the man who documented the rise of the Blues, early Rock-and-Roll days, the Negro Leagues, Dr. Martin Luther King Jr. and the Civil Rights Movement.

To my surprise, Milly said I should call Ernest and pay him a visit at his studio on Beale Street. I couldn't believe my ears. Within minutes I was on the phone with the unofficial mayor of Memphis and we became fast friends. As it turned out, my visit to meet Ernest Withers coincided with the 2002 W. C. Handy Awards for the best in Blues music. (In 2006, the Handy Awards were renamed the Blues Music Awards.) I watched Otis Taylor win the Best New Artist and Acoustic Blues Album of the Year for "White African," Keb' Mo' win Acoustic Blues Artist of the Year, and B.B. King win Blues Entertainer of the Year. Ike Turner was there to receive Comeback Blues Album of the Year for "Here and Now." Etta James won for Soul/Blues Female Artist of the Year. I thought that I had died and gone to Blues Heaven when independent label Sun Records founder Sam Phillips and "Miss Rhythm" Ruth Brown took to the stage. I was watching living history and was getting driven around town by a living legend.

Ernest Withers had documented the rise of many of the early days Blues and Rock and Roll artists. But he also served to freeze frame the abyss in American race history.

Withers documented the Emmitt Till trial about the fourteen-year-old Chicago boy who allegedly flirted with a 21-year-old married white woman, Carolyn Bryant, in Bryant's Grocery and Meat Market in Money, Mississippi. Four days later, Emmitt Till was abducted in the middle of the night from the home of his uncle, Reverend Moses Wright, beaten and shot to death by Carolyn's husband Roy Bryant and accomplices. His body was found in the Tallahatchie River, weighted down by a 75-pound cotton gin fan. The Emmitt Till murder in late August 1955 was one of the galvanizing moments for the American Civil Rights

Movement, especially since his mother elected to bury him in an open casket. "I wanted the world to see what they did to my baby."[69] *Jet* magazine and the local black newspaper the *Chicago Defender* documented the trial and funeral using photographs that included those from Ernest Withers. A hasty trial by an all-white male jury acquitted Roy Bryant and his main accomplice, half-brother J. W. Milam, in just a little over an hour. One juror said, "If we hadn't stopped to drink pop, it wouldn't have taken that long."[70]

As an African-American photojournalist, Withers was not allowed to sit with the white photographers from the major media who were covering the murder trial of Bryant and Milam. Withers was relegated to the back of the courtroom in a cordoned off space just for him and other non-white media. Ernest told me that he had learned his photography craft as a Army staff photographer in World War II, but he was not allowed to pull over white drivers while serving as a police officer in late 1940s and 1950s Mississippi. If he saw a white drunk driver weaving along the road, he had to call for white back up to arrest the violator.

Ernest drove me around Memphis and talked in language that reflected a man of his time: acronyms like "BI" (before integration) and "AI" (after integration). We ate in a black restaurant that was among the most popular blacks only "BI" eatery in Memphis. I felt privileged to be in the company of this man. I even tried to make a documentary film about the life of Ernest C. Withers, with backing from my friends at Tree Media Company in Santa Monica, California but it never came to fruition. I wanted every school kid in America to have a chance to listen to this man tell his American story using his own vernacular.

---

[69] This is a recollection of Brookings Institution senior fellow and author Joyce Ladner, who made this comment at a panel discussion hosted by Brookings called "Race: The Great American Divide," in January 2000. See http://www.brookings.edu/events/2000/0111race.aspx?rssid=race

[70] Albert Alschuler, "Racial Quotas and the Jury," *Duke Law Journal* 44, 4 (1995): 706.

While visiting with Ernest on Beale Street, I was struck by how many international people came by to pay homage to him and his work. To these people from afar, Ernest was someone to be admired and privileged to meet. There was a couple from Canada and I was told many came from as far away as Europe. Those who visited said that they loved American history and culture, including its songs, cuisine, lifestyle, and language. I wondered why it took people from outside our own culture to tell us how rich it was. Even more, I wondered how many black and white school kids in Memphis might not have even heard about Ernest Withers. Sadly, Ernest passed on October 15, 2007 at the age of 85, just a month after I left for a semester's teaching at Tsinghua University in Beijing, China.[71] His legacy continues in the millions of photographs he took that preserve our history and culture. His work will hopefully receive its due respect in the yet unopened National Museum of African American History and Culture in Washington, DC, part of the Smithsonian Institution museums.

We are a nation that needs a Ministry of American Culture or something similar to celebrate our heritage to the rest of the world. We have so many war memorials. Why not memorials to our famous artists, writers, and singers? I long for us to tell our collective stories to the world. Once bitten with the American history bug, you are never quite the same. Legendary music producer Quincy Jones spoke about the need for a presidentially-appointed secretary of the arts during his December 2008 book tour for his memoir, *The Complete Quincy Jones: My Life and Passions*, emphasizing his point with the charge that the U.S. is the only country without one.[72] By that, he means that the U.S. is the only major industrialized democracy without a Ministry of Culture. Consider how other countries fund the arts in comparison to the

---

[71] Michael Lollar, "Ernest Withers dies at 85: Photographer with a great heart had 'burning desire to shoot pictures,'" *Memphis Commercial Appeal*, October 16, 2007.

[72] http://www.marinij.com/lifestyles/ci_11267819

U.S. Government. The National Endowment for the Arts explains that in "countries like France, Germany, Mexico, or China, most arts funding comes from the government—either at a federal or local level. For the most part, these systems tend to be centralized, often located in a large ministry of culture.... The subsidies awarded by ministries of culture are enormous by American standards. For example, the government subvention for Italy's major opera houses is nearly ten times larger than the annual Arts Endowment working budget."[73] The U.S. has no overarching central Ministry of Culture because of our long tradition of decentralization and the free market system. Just 13% of public subsidies go toward funding of nonprofit arts groups in our local communities. Until and unless we make a concerted change to use taxpayer monies to support art and culture, we'll continue to rely on the for-profit marketplace to determine our cultural content. In the meantime, our traditional American music genres in jazz, blues, folk, Big Band, soul, country, bluegrass, and musical theater will continue to go begging for financial support. How many young people in America eschew these genres for the American Idol® punch ticket?

Writer Rick Bragg explains the American longing for our cultural heritage in his New York Times' travel piece, "Driving the Blues Trail, in Search of a Lost Muse."

> *I came looking for the blues. I came to hear a big woman rattle the windows with a voice like a hurricane spinning at the bottom of a well, to hear a skinny man sing about big-legged women and unworthy husbands, to eat cornbread and collards, to have a gospel choir on the radio snatch me up in the rapture as I speed through the green, flat country.*

---

[73] Dana Gioia, Chairman, National Endowment for the Arts, Preface, *National Endowment for the Arts: How the United States Funds the Arts*. Second Edition. Published by the National Endowment for the Arts Office of Research & Analysis, Sunil Iyengar, Director. Washington, DC, January 2007.

> *I came to see this land where the blues began, and to see a child who was born here pick up a guitar and plug in a hot amplifier with a sound like bacon spitting from a hot skillet, and play me a song.*
>
> *It's got it all. I had to hunt hard for some of it, because the legendary Delta where Robert Johnson and Muddy Waters played every day in a home-brew haze at fish frys and juke joints is long gone—and perhaps never was. Live blues can be hard to find in most towns, the juke joints killed by crack cocaine and indifference.*[74]

I know what Bragg means about a lost muse. Other artists inspire writers. We get oxygen from poetry, old country store conversation, lyrics and musical rhythms. We've got an incredible opportunity to celebrate America's richness to the world with the election of our first African-American president. He's a man who loves history and undoubtedly its music, culture, and cuisine. How could he not? He's a Chicago man.

I'm a Southerner. Growing up, I've often heard it said, "American by birth, Southern by the grace of God." This statement can be taken in two ways. To some, it might offend. The South has had a dark history in race relations. There's no doubt about it. But I am a white woman with a Native American heritage (Mohawk and Creek) who has benefited from my racial understanding because of my Southern heritage. I have learned more about black history and its contributions to American culture because of my love of Southern writers, artists, and Southern food, all heavily influenced by the Black experience. I have Native American heritage in blood and the Black experience in my soul. This sensitivity is not to say that I really know what it means to be black in America. I can never know that completely, but I remain an open and active listener and

---

[74] Rick Bragg, "Driving the Blues Trail, In Search of a Lost Muse," *The New York Times*, April 19, 2002.

observer of all the diverse life experiences that America brings to the table everyday.

To paraphrase the soul singer James Brown, whose hometown of Augusta, Georgia is my city of birth, *I feel good* about our new president and what he may do for renewed interest and appreciation in American history and culture. Obama is in the catbird seat to explain and influence what is America to the world. But he alone cannot restore America's good reputation around the world. We must make ourselves gifts to the world and open up our eyes and ears to learn from what the world has to teach us. Then we'll just let President Obama come along for the victory ride.

www.ingramcontent.com/pod-product-compliance
Lightning Source LLC
Chambersburg PA
CBHW081418270326
41931CB00015B/3326

* 9 7 8 1 9 3 4 8 4 0 8 1 8 *